# DEADLY DILEMMA

## A CAPT. CYNDI STAFFORD NOVEL

# DEADLY DILEMMA

### A CAPT. CYNDI STAFFORD NOVEL

# DAN STRATMAN

# ALSO BY DAN STRATMAN

# DEDICATION

*To my sainted Mother, Jan. Your kind heart and
unending patience with family and friends were just a
few of your admirable personality traits that I strive to
hopefully emulate one day.*

# CHAPTER 1

"GHOST TWO-SIX, YOU are cleared for takeoff on runway nine and a high-speed flyby."

The young fighter pilot grinned broadly under his oxygen mask after receiving permission to unleash his inner Tom Cruise on the unsuspecting people beneath his flight path. He pressed the microphone button on the throttle. "Ghost Two-Six cleared for takeoff." He chuckled to himself, "This should get their attention."

Controllers in the tower at Cheyenne Regional Airport rushed to the window facing west, eager to watch what was about to happen across the other side of Interstate 25.

The pilot stood on the brake pedals and advanced the throttle in his F-35. Knowing they wouldn't restrain the $120 million beast any longer, he released the brakes, dropped his heels to the floor, and mashed the throttle into full afterburner.

The Pratt & Whitney engine went from an angry howl to an earth-shaking roar. Like an oversize blowtorch, flames twice the length of the jet shot out of the tailpipe. The F-35 Lightning II leaped forward like a predator pouncing on its prey.

A mile away, windows in the tower cab rattled in their metal frames. Airport workers on the ramp tightly cupped their hands over their ears. The impact of the sound waves caused their chest walls to pulsate. The heads of every pilot snapped toward the unmistakable sound of the afterburner, secretly wishing they were in the cockpit.

Less than half the runway was needed to get airborne. The pilot scooped up the gear and retracted the flaps. He leveled off a mere one hundred feet above the smattering of buildings in the capital city.

The fighter accelerated at the ludicrous rate of an additional one hundred knots every five seconds until it reached Mach .99. The "Maverick" wannabe eased the throttle back just enough to prevent his permanent grounding for shattering every window in town. The pilot banked right into a wide, looping turn back toward the north. He looked over his shoulder, acquired his target, and smiled.

The stealthy gray fighter hugged the snow-covered terrain as it snuck up on its target. The fighter jock reached out and raised the red safety cover over the MASTER ARM switch. Bomb bay doors snapped open. He sat up a little straighter in his ejection seat and rocked his head side to side to ease the tension in his neck. The pilot rolled out of the turn and pointed the nose of the jet directly at F. E. Warren Air Force Base, home of the 90th Nuclear Missile Wing.

———◆———

A late-model blue sedan pulled into the specially marked spot in front of the base gymnasium. One large silver star was the only thing on the license plate. In the back seat, hidden from view by darkly tinted windows, was the lone passenger.

The driver zipped up his parka and jumped out of the car, scurrying around to the right side. He moved quickly but kept a gloved hand on the car as he navigated the slippery pavement. The driver pulled the door open and stood at attention.

Brigadier General Arthur McNeil stepped out of his

staff car and took in a deep breath of crisp Wyoming air. McNeil was two inches shorter than Napoleon Bonaparte and had a high-and-tight haircut. At fifty-three, he wasn't reluctant to wear a tight-fitting track suit to show off his muscular, sinewy build. He waited at the back of the car as his driver popped open the trunk. General McNeil reached in and pulled out his gym bag. A silver star adorned the side.

An airman glued to his cell phone strolled past the front of the car. He was watching videos of skateboarders wiping out as they tried new tricks.

McNeil saw him and yelled, "A-ten-hut!"

Fresh from eight weeks of basic training in San Antonio, the eighteen-year-old instinctively snapped to attention and stared straight ahead. McNeil's bright red face soon filled his view.

Inches from the perplexed airman's face, McNeil barked, "Son, this isn't the Army. We have standards in the Air Force. When you see a staff car with the license plate of a flag officer attached, you *will* salute it."

The teenager furrowed his brow and looked around nervously. "But sir, I didn't see anyone in the car."

"I don't give a damn if my car is at the bottom of a lake. If you see it, you salute it!" McNeil's face reddened even more. "Give your name and unit information to my driver. Your commanding officer will be hearing from me!" McNeil stomped off.

As he marched up the sidewalk, a gray object streaked silently overhead from behind—at 99 percent of the speed of sound.

A quarter second later, the sound caught up to it.

The terrifying, thunderous roar sounded like it was coming from an unholy, pissed-off mechanical angel of death. It caused the frozen ground to tremble.

Car alarms across the base started wailing.

Snow that had been resting peacefully on tree branches

fell off in large clumps.

McNeil's heart skipped a beat when the powerful shock wave smacked him in the back of the head. He instinctively ducked for cover. When he worked up the courage to look up, he swore he could hear laughter coming from the departing plane. McNeil thrust his middle finger skyward as the pilot pulled the F-35 up into a crushing eight-G vertical climb. Obscenities that spewed from his mouth were drowned out by the deafening noise.

# CHAPTER 2

WITH THE MOCK attack safely over, McNeil looked around to see if anyone had seen him cower down on the concrete. Anyone who did knew enough to pretend not to notice. He straightened up, resumed a cocksure posture, and started for the gym door.

Air Force regulation tan paint on the rundown, drab building was peeling and flaking off. Its roof sagged slightly under the heavy snow load. In contrast, a bright new sign on the front wall displayed the patch of the Global Strike Command. It was the latest in a long series of Major Command signs that had hung in that same spot, beginning with the vaunted Strategic Air Command.

Fort D.A. Russell was originally established as a cavalry post in 1867 during the later stages of the American Indian Wars. It was a desolate outpost on what was then considered the western frontier of the country. The Army had constructed it to protect workers building the Transcontinental Railroad for the Union Pacific. Over the years, Fort Russell had played host to units of infantry, cavalry, and field artillery—eventually converting to an Air Force base.

Now named F. E. Warren AFB, in honor of a former governor, it had been placed on the National Register of Historic Places decades ago.

The small base was easily the oldest continuously active military installation in the Air Force. It had the dubious distinction of being the only active base without a runway.

Its current mission was to operate launch control centers buried sixty feet underground. They controlled 150 Minuteman III nuclear missile silos scattered across the region where Wyoming, Colorado, and Nebraska intersect. If World War III ever were to kick off, much of the ensuing global nuclear destruction would launch from F. E. Warren units.

Still fuming from the pilot's brazen stunt, McNeil flung open the heavy metal door to the gym. A wide foyer covered in faded emerald-green linoleum led up to the front desk.

The attendant working behind the desk saw McNeil coming and shook his head. He forced a smile and said, "Good morning, General."

McNeil ignored his greeting. "Aren't there normally two people working the morning shift? Where's the cute redhead who works here?"

The man leaned on the counter and nonchalantly shrugged. "Couldn't tell you, sir. She must be in the bathroom."

"That figures." McNeil walked off. Before rounding the corner, he turned his head and shouted, "I'm not to be disturbed for any reason!"

After the sound of his footsteps faded away, a young red-headed woman slowly peeked her head above the Formica counter. "Is he gone?"

Her coworker looked down the hallway and checked. "You're safe. I'll let you know if I see him coming back this way."

McNeil stopped at the door to a large exercise studio. A sign on the glass read: *Missileer Mandatory Martial Arts Training Class – 0800.* He opened the door and strode confidently in.

The room reeked of sweat and body odor that had

permeated the wood floor over decades of use. A large, padded mat covered the floor in the front of the room.

When the general entered, the small talk immediately ceased. Everyone moved to spots an arm's length apart.

McNeil positioned himself in the center of the first row, six inches from the man who was standing there. He quickly took the hint and moved to the back of the room. The general dropped his gym bag where the man had been standing. *BG A. MCNEIL* was embroidered on the side.

At exactly 0800, a beautiful blonde quietly slipped unnoticed through the door. Her long silky hair was pulled back in a ponytail. She stood at the back of the room and studied the crowd with her crystal-blue eyes, sizing up each person. Satisfied she understood whom she was up against, the woman threaded her way to the front of the room and positioned herself on the large mat. She was in her midtwenties, five-foot-eleven in her bare feet, and wore a crisply starched white *gi* encircled with a black belt. The loose-fitting garment concealed a body that was muscular but feminine, sculpted but soft. In other words, deceptively dangerous. "Good morning, Missileers. Welcome to martial arts training."

The one-star cocked his head in confusion. "Where's the instructor? Is he running late?"

She forced a smile. "No, sir, *he's* not running late. I'm the instructor."

"You?" the general scoffed.

"In the flesh."

"You're in the wrong room, Miss. This isn't yoga class. I specifically directed that someone trained in martial arts teach these classes."

"I believe I'm more than qualified, General McNeil. I help the owner of a studio in Cheyenne teach judo to kids. And I—"

"Kids?" the general scoffed. "Our enemies aren't *chil-*

*dren.*" He turned to the group. "Listen up. I was sent to this godforsaken base to clean up the mess left by your last three commanders. You people are expected to be warriors. It's about damned time you start thinking and acting like it. This class is just a start. Fat and weak will no longer be acceptable at my base. Every month, there will be mandatory fitness testing and weigh-ins."

Heads sagged among those officers in the room still holding on to a little extra baby fat.

"Missileers who don't measure up will have their promotions put on indefinite hold until you get with the program. The days of the Global Strike Command being considered the red-headed stepchild by the jet jocks running the Air Force ends as of now." He turned back. "Miss, teaching children sure as hell doesn't qualify you—"

"I also studied krav maga with a Mossad agent when my dad was on an exchange tour with the Israeli Air Force. And I have a black belt in judo. Oh wait, I almost forgot. I was on the US Taekwondo team at the last Olympics. But if you're willing to wait, I'd be happy to try and find a *guy* who's more qualified to lead this class." The young woman crossed her arms and glared at the diminutive man. "Sir."

The general's face flushed with anger. His pinched expression left no doubt he didn't appreciate being embarrassed in front of the class. "That won't be necessary." His eyes narrowed. "Proceed, Miss…?"

"I'm Capt. Cyndi Stafford. I'm a missile combat crew commander and instructor here at F. E. Warren."

"Are you now?" He looked Cyndi up and down like a piece of meat. "That means you serve under me, if I remember correctly how the chain of command functions."

"I work *for* you; that's correct."

"Your name is Stafford?"

"Yes, sir."

"Are you related to the infamous test pilot Brock Stafford?"

"He's my father," she responded proudly.

McNeil stroked his chin and nodded slowly. "So...you're in the Air Force, Stafford is your father, yet here you are, a missileer. Interesting." A smarmy grin formed on his face. "He must be very *proud*." His last word was soaked in sarcasm.

Cyndi felt like lashing out but held her tongue.

His annoying grin evaporated. "How is the old bastard enjoying civilian life these days?"

"He's dead."

# CHAPTER 3

A N AWKWARD SILENCE fell over the room.
A strained expression crossed the general's face as he searched his mind for some way to save face after her unexpected response.

"Why don't we get started? Then you can decide if my class is what you have in mind," Cyndi volunteered, giving the one-star an out.

"You can count on it. You have my permission to proceed."

Cyndi paced the mat with the confidence of a model working a fashion runway in Paris. She looked out at the group. "I'll begin by demonstrating how to handle the two situations you are most likely to encounter. The first is when someone is rushing at you—being on the defensive—and the second is when *you* are the aggressor."

Men in the class were more gawking at her than listening to her self-defense instruction.

She looked at McNeil. "I'll need a volunteer for my first demonstration." Cyndi paused for a beat then lifted her hand, pointing at the man standing directly behind him. "How about you?"

"Me?" The man looked around, positive Cyndi was talking about someone else.

"Yes, you." Cyndi had chosen the biggest guy in the room. "What's your name?"

"First Lt. Terrance Washington, ma'am. But I think it would be better if you choose someone else."

"Don't worry, big man, I won't hurt you."

He chuckled. "It's not that, ma'am. I played linebacker for the Bulldogs in college. I outweigh you by a hundred pounds, and well…"

"Well…what?"

"I'd hate to mess up your lovely makeup, that's all," he said smugly.

The class snickered at his misogynistic remark.

McNeil turned and joined in.

Cyndi waved him forward. "Come on up, and let's see what you've got."

He shrugged. "Okay. Don't say I didn't warn you." Washington strolled confidently onto the mat and squared off ten feet away from Cyndi.

She turned her back to the man. "I want you to run up and grab me from behind. Pretend I'm a quarterback scrambling out of the pocket, if that helps." Cyndi spread her feet shoulder width apart, equally distributing her weight. She crouched slightly.

The big man rushed at her like an angry Brahman bull.

Cyndi ducked, spun to the left, and swept her right leg across his shins.

The cocky former jock went airborne. He slammed face-first into the mat with an embarrassing thud.

Cyndi knelt next to him, snatched his right wrist, and pinned it back against his spine. She yanked his wrist higher and higher until he let out a sharp yelp. Payback delivered, she released his wrist and stood up. "As I've just demonstrated, skill and surprise—not size or gender—are what counts against your opponent. When you find yourself up against a person who is bigger and stronger than you, using their momentum against them is a highly effective countermove." She reached down and held out a conciliatory hand. "How's my makeup?"

The big guy reluctantly took her hand and got on his feet. "Fine, ma'am," he mumbled under his breath. He slinked back to his spot, pinching his bloody nose.

Cyndi held back a smile as she continued. "Next, I'll demonstrate a move to incapacitate your opponent when you are on the offensive. General McNeil, would you like to volunteer?"

McNeil was incensed at Cyndi having the audacity to challenge him in front of his troops. But having given her permission to teach the class, he couldn't risk looking like a coward by refusing to spar with her.

All eyes were on the one-star.

"I'll volunteer."

McNeil turned to see the man standing next to him raising his hand. Relief coursed through his tense body. "Since I was raised to never hurt a lady…"—he waved the man up toward the mat—"I'll let this fine young man stand in for me."

"I guess you'll do," Cyndi said, disappointment evident in her voice. "What's your name?"

"Second Lt. Lance Garcia, ma'am. Dallas, Texas."

He was a native of the Lone Star State and felt it imperative that everyone knew that.

Lance had a lanky build and stood six feet, two inches tall. He didn't have any problem getting dates. His rugged, handsome looks and deep brown eyes had already earned him the starring role in two Air Force recruiting commercials during his short tenure in the military.

Lance nervously approached the mat. "Where should I stand?" he asked, swallowing hard.

Cyndi pointed. "Stand there and put your hands up in a defensive position. I'm going to come at you, and you try to stop me."

"Yes, ma'am." Lance stood straight legged and put his hands up like he was praying.

Cyndi rolled her eyes and exhaled loudly. "No, not like that." She went over and pulled his hands apart. "Spread your hands shoulder width apart and crouch down slightly to distribute your weight."

He did his best to prepare for Cyndi's attack, silently rethinking the wisdom of trying to impress the general by volunteering.

She backed up ten feet then ran full speed at her trembling opponent.

In the blink of an eye, Lance latched on to her wrists, fell on his back, and used his feet to send Cyndi up and over the top of him. She landed on her back with a thud.

A collective gasp came from the room.

Lance sprang up off the mat and turned to face Cyndi. His hands were poised to strike, and he was crouched down in a perfect defensive position.

"Just like I thought," McNeil said loudly.

Lance straightened up and raced over, offering her his hand. "Are you hurt?"

"I'm *fine!*" Cyndi refused to accept his hand. She got up and dusted herself off. Ego definitely bruised, she grudgingly said, "That was very impressive. I suspect you've had some martial arts training."

Lance shrugged. "Maybe a little. I did watch a lot of Jackie Chan movies when I was a kid, though. I probably just got lucky."

Cyndi didn't appreciate his irreverent sense of humor. "Very funny. Let's try that again." She squared up and came at Lance again.

This time, she easily took him down. Cyndi ended up on top of Lance as he lay on his back, straddling him and pinning his hands to the mat.

From the pleased look on his face, he didn't seem to mind being in that position. "Not bad for a yoga instructor," he said with a wink. "When's your next class?"

She released his hands and straightened up. "That move you made the first round was very impressive." Cyndi sat back and deliberately plopped all her weight down on his stomach. Air rushed from his lungs. She crossed her arms and smiled innocently. "Well done."

"Thanks, so was yours," Lance replied through gritted teeth as he struggled to draw in a breath. "But unfortunately, it wasn't quite enough. Looks like I won round two as well."

Cyndi recoiled back. "You must have hit your head, Lieutenant. Clearly, I won the second round."

"I guess that all depends on your perspective."

"And what perspective could that possibly be?" she asked incredulously.

"Well, the way I see it, the first round I swept a beautiful woman off her feet. The second time I had her on top of me, pinning my hands down." His perfect, pearl-white teeth flashed in her face as he grinned broadly. "Feels like a double win to me."

Cyndi rolled her eyes and groaned. "You need to up your game, Lieutenant Garcia. Your pickup lines need serious work." She jumped to her feet and straightened her gi. "Are you always so cocky?"

He stood and dusted himself off. "Not always." Lance ran his fingers through his thick black hair. "Only when I send an Olympian to the mat."

At hearing his brash remark, Cyndi's temper got the best of her. "All right pretty boy, let's go again." She got set in an offensive stance. "Best two out of three."

Lance shrugged. "If you insist." He stepped back ten feet, raised up his hands in exactly the right position, and flashed a sly grin. "But I must warn you, I did teach judo to kids for a few years."

Cyndi cocked her head at the cryptic comment. "So, you *have* had—"

Suddenly, a red light mounted on the wall began flashing.

A young lieutenant rushed into the room. "General McNeil, there you are. You need to come with me immediately." He bent down, resting his hands on his knees while he gulped down much needed oxygen. "North Korea just launched a nuclear missile at the US."

McNeil didn't think twice. He snatched his gym bag and ran for the door. "Everyone report to your squadron and await further instructions." He grabbed the lieutenant's arm. "Where is the missile headed?"

"Los Angeles, sir."

Cyndi reacted in horror. "Oh my God. My mom lives in LA!"

# CHAPTER 4

*Twenty minutes earlier*

COLONEL STANLEY WILMER, forty-seven, balding and carrying an ample spare tire, stood at the glass wall separating his office from the floor of the F. E. Warren command post.

The high-tech nerve center that monitored real-time, real-world threats—a fixture of every Air Force base worldwide—had three giant screens on the far wall that dominated the large, well-lit space. They displayed data ranging from the local weather to the location of every one of the 150 Minuteman III missiles under its control. Personnel at dozens of workstations busied themselves with routine tasks meant to divert their attention while they waited for the alert they hoped would never come.

Wilmer flinched at the sound of a jet streaking overhead at rooftop level. He looked up and yelled at the ceiling. "Damned jet jocks!" He walked over to his desk and picked up a white envelope. He ripped it open and quickly scanned the letter. His enthusiastic expression slowly melted away as he read. When he finished, he shook his head in disgust. "If they don't know real talent when they see it, screw the Air Force." The colonel sat down, crumpled up the letter, and spiked it into the trash can. Wilmer plopped his feet up and stabbed at the remote to change channels on his TV.

He stopped to watch a grizzled foreign reporter with

CNN doing a remote from the DMZ in South Korea. With cartoonishly long binoculars, soldiers in an observation tower on the north side of the border kept a close watch on the reporter and his cameraman.

When the red light on the camera came on, the reporter switched to a suitably serious expression. "Intelligence sources released satellite images yesterday that show renewed activity at a plutonium reprocessing plant outside of Pyongyang, North Korea. The UN has denounced the provocative actions of the communist state as a clear violation of Security Council resolutions." He flipped the page on his spiral notebook. "In related news, the Korean Central News Agency, mouthpiece for the regime, reported that last week a high-ranking government official was executed. In a barbaric twist—even for this regime—he was publicly executed before a stadium crowd. In fact, he was tied to a post and shot with explosive flak rounds from an anti-aircraft gun while his family was forced to watch." The reporter cleared his throat. He closed his notebook and continued. "The official's supposed crime? Disrespecting Supreme Leader Kim Jong Un by slouching during a meeting presided over by the dictator. Just another tragic and grisly reminder, say White House and intelligence officials, of the kind of brutal atrocities this regime uses to maintain its deadly grip on power. Back to you in the studio."

Master Sgt. Mark Holmes, the Non-Commissioned Officer in Charge (NCOIC) of the command post, stood outside the colonel's office and knocked on the door.

Wilmer quickly pulled his feet off the desk and grabbed a handful of papers. "Enter," he said angrily.

Holmes walked up to the front of Wilmer's desk and stood at attention. "Shift change checklist is complete, sir." He held out an SD card. "This is the recording of all activity from last shift."

Every piece of equipment in the command post

was connected to an IBM mainframe located in a cli-
mate-controlled room. Even though the computer was
over twenty years old, it was considered "new" in the
perennially underfunded Global Strike Command.

Every phone call, computer keystroke, and the operational status of the fleet of LGM-30G Minuteman III
Inter-Continental Ballistic Missiles (ICBMs) tucked into
silos across the region were recorded onto a high-capac-
ity secure digital card each shift.

Wilmer snatched the card out of his hand then looked
at his wristwatch. "Shift change occurs at 0800, sergeant,
not 0801. Don't let it happen again."

As he unlocked his desk drawer, Wilmer's phone rang.
He picked up the handset, listened for a moment, then
said, "Hello, dear…nothing…same old thing. Wait, there's
someone in my office…hang on." The full-bird colonel
cradled the handset against his shoulder and fished an SD
card from the drawer. "Here." He handed it to Holmes
then locked the drawer. "Get back to work." He flicked
his wrist and waved his NCOIC away with the back of
his hand.

Holmes slammed the door when he left the office.

Before Wilmer could continue, his wife rattled off
her newest list of grievances. He listened to the one-
way conversation and occasionally nodded. He removed
his glasses and cleaned the lenses with his tie. The colonel picked up the remote again and flipped through the
channels. Every few minutes he tossed in a "yes, dear."
During a rare moment when his wife was taking a breath,
Wilmer interjected, "I got the letter from the promotion
board."

Silence on the other end lasted a mere two seconds. It
was broken with a pointed demand. "Well, don't make
me wait all day. Did you get a star or not?"

"The promotion board passed me over again. At my
level, it's either up or out. That means I have four months

and seven days to go. But who's counting." He flipped channels on the TV while listening to his wife berate him for not making the rank of brigadier general.

Suddenly, the base klaxon sounded. Red lights flashed throughout the command post. Personnel collided with each other as they scrambled to get back to their desks.

Wilmer jumped up from his chair and tried to end the conversation. "I have to go. There's an alert...Yes, I'll pick up a gallon...No, I won't forget." Finally, he slammed the handset down. Colonel Wilmer ran out onto the floor of the command post and took up his position overseeing the room. "Battle stations!"

# CHAPTER 5

THE WELL-TRAINED STAFF went to work.
Sergeant Holmes took his position next to Colonel Wilmer. "Stations, report your status," he barked.

Before they could report, a loudspeaker mounted on the wall blared a startling message. "This is an Emergency Action Message from the National Command Authority. Time is 1509 Zulu. NORAD has detected the launch of a long-range nuclear missile from the territory of North Korea. Target is Los Angeles, California. Estimated time of impact is twenty-nine minutes. Stand by for—"

The loudspeaker went dead.

The large displays at the front of the room flashed then went black.

A second later, the entire room went dark.

Emergency lighting fixtures mounted in each corner of the room kicked in.

"What the hell is going on?" Wilmer asked, with panic in his voice.

"Stations, report your status!" Holmes yelled.

One by one, people in the room announced the bad news.

"Satellite comms are down."

"Landlines, down."

"Unable to verify authenticity of EAM with the National Command Authority."

"Backup generator coming online in one minute."

Wilmer grabbed a young lieutenant nearby. "Go find

General McNeil, and bring him back here immediately." He looked at his watch. "Check the gym first. He's probably there."

The man sprinted off.

Holmes pointed toward the entrance. "Security, close and secure the doors."

A hulking airman in full battle dress and armed with an M-16 closed the doors to the command post and stood guard outside.

Holmes turned to the colonel. "What are your orders, sir?"

A bead of sweat rolled down his chubby face. "I can't...I need more information. Get the Pentagon on the line."

"Sir, all comms are down."

"Then we'll wait for General McNeil to get here. He'll know what to do."

"Sir, that could take too long. I need your orders now."

Wilmer began hyperventilating. "The bastards must have decapitated the entire command structure. Oh my God! They're probably outside the building right now." Wilmer had a death grip on the handrail. "Start...start the nuclear retaliation checklist."

All activity ceased. The room went dead silent. The staff couldn't believe what they'd just heard.

Holmes put both hands up like stop signs. "Slow down, Colonel. We don't know if the Emergency Action Message is authentic or not. This could be just another exercise testing our response time. Let's try to contact NORAD and find out what's going on. I'll go get my phone from my car and call them."

No electronic devices, including personal phones, where allowed in the secure command post. A simple cell phone out in the parking lot had become the only way to contact the vast, trillion-dollar military apparatus.

Wilmer tried in vain to get his breathing under control while he considered the advice of his NCOIC. "No.

That's not protocol. There are clear-cut procedures in place for how to respond in a decapitation scenario. Start the—"

Holmes shocked the colonel by grabbing his arm. "Stanley, listen to me. You can't make that decision yet. Something doesn't feel right about this. We don't know if there is a missile on its way or if there is some sort of glitch in the system. We have twenty-eight thousand of our own people stationed in South Korea. Anyone still alive after we nuke North Korea will die within a week from radiation poisoning."

Wilmer yanked his arm away. "Get your hand off me. I have a sworn duty to follow orders and make the difficult decision when the time comes. The American people have put their trust in me. I don't intend to let them down." He turned to the hushed room and cleared his throat. "Start the nuclear retaliation checklist. Launch ten missiles. Target is North Korea."

# CHAPTER 6

LIKE A GOOD airman, Master Sergeant Holmes followed the terrifying order. He took a deep breath then released it. "All stations, listen up. On the orders of Colonel Wilmer, initiate the nuclear retaliation checklist. This is not a drill. I say again, initiate the nuclear retaliation checklist."

Airmen manning each desk pulled binders with red-striped borders from shelves above their workstation. The spines bore the chilling words, *TOP SECRET – NUCLEAR RETALIATION CHECKLIST.*

Tamper-proof tape sealing the binders was ripped off. Quivering fingers traced down through the checklists as the airmen executed each step. This helped ensure they didn't miss anything on their march down the path to Armageddon. With no ability to get confirmation from higher authority, the staff operated in the blind and hoped the procedures in the binders—written back when SAC oversaw nuclear missiles—still worked.

Step by step, they methodically prepared to unleash a nuclear apocalypse on twenty-five million unsuspecting people living on the northern half of the Korean Peninsula.

———◆———

General McNeil burst into the building. He marched down the hall toward the command post entrance. His driver and the lieutenant who'd fetched him from the gym trailed closely behind.

The guard saw a small man dressed in a track suit coming his way. He lowered his rifle and shouted, "Halt! This is a restricted area. Stop or you will be fired upon."

The driver and the lieutenant dove for the floor and covered their heads.

McNeil charged ahead.

The guard racked his gun and aimed it at the man's chest. "I'm warning you. Stop!"

Now only ten feet away, McNeil yelled, "You moron, unless you want to spend the rest of your tour locked up in Leavenworth, I order you to stand down!"

The confused airman leaned forward and squinted to get a better look at the onrushing civilian. He finally recognized his boss. "General...McNeil?"

McNeil slapped the barrel of the gun aside and stormed into the command post. Personnel were frantically preparing for launch.

"Colonel Wilmer, I'm assuming command. Status update. Now!"

Wilmer rushed over to the entrance. "Sir, we got an Emergency Action Message saying the North Koreans have launched a missile at Los Angeles. Before I could verify it, we lost all connections to the National Command Authority. I've implemented retaliation protocol targeting North Korea. Ten missiles are ready."

"Excellent job, Colonel." A disturbing look spread across McNeil's face. "Continue with the launch checklist."

The airmen turned back around and continued their checklists. When completed, they closed their binders.

Less than a minute later, Wilmer announced, "Missiles ready for launch, sir."

Suddenly, the overhead lighting came back on. The screens at the front of the room came alive. The information presented on them looked like any other day.

Telephones at workstations began ringing off the hook.

"What's happening?" McNeil asked.

"The emergency generator must have come online, sir," Wilmer volunteered.

"Launch the missiles," McNeil ordered.

"Stop! Stop the launch!" Sergeant Holmes rushed up waving an SD card.

Every head in the room turned toward him.

"It's a training exercise! This isn't a blank card you gave me. It has a decapitation scenario training exercise on it. There is no attack!"

Colonel Wilmer grabbed the SD card. His mouth dropped open when he read the warning label printed on the card.

McNeil exploded. "Dammit!"

Everyone nearby looked away, hoping that avoiding eye contact would prevent them from being the target of his rage.

"How the hell could you mistake a training scenario card for a blank card, Wilmer!" McNeil pushed him aside and rushed forward. "Stand down! Terminate launch checklists!"

Sergeant Holmes repeated the same command at each workstation, verifying that the missiles had indeed been put back to standby status.

The worst part of the fiasco was that the command post had been transmitting its preparation to launch a salvo of nukes to the entire military command structure. The supposed blackout in the command post had been part of the training exercise. Until the SD card had been yanked out of the mainframe, every other branch of the military believed World War III was starting.

McNeil got right in Wilmer's face. "I want to know how the hell this happened!"

The dressing down was interrupted by an enlisted man

holding up a phone at a nearby desk. "General, the office of the Joint Chiefs of Staff is calling. They're demanding to know what is going on out here."

Soon other staff held up their phones.

"Cheyenne Mountain is calling."

"Raven Rock is on the line, sir."

"Headquarters is on the encrypted hotline."

McNeil's eyes filled with fire. He turned and poked Wilmer in the chest. "I'll be damned if I'm going to let a loser like you destroy my career. I'm holding you personally responsible. You created this friggin' mess, Colonel, you clean it up. Be in my office in thirty minutes with a full report." McNeil turned to leave but then suddenly stopped. He spun back around and stood there, arms crossed.

Wilmer let out a feeble sigh and saluted. "Yes, sir."

# CHAPTER 7

CYNDI AND LANCE hustled up the snow-covered sidewalk toward the entrance to a dated, two-story brick building—home of the 322nd Missile Squadron. They had identical military-issue camouflage-pattern backpacks slung over their shoulders. The packs contained everything needed to go on short-notice alert in case of an emergency. A flight suit, boots, underwear, socks, and most importantly, three days' worth of high-calorie energy bars were in their bags.

Lance opened the door for her. They turned left and hurried down the hallway with their fellow missileers.

Cyndi cut in front of Lance and walked backward. "You lied to me."

"Sounds like someone's ego got a little bruised at the gym," he quipped.

"You *have* had martial arts training, haven't you?"

He tried to maneuver around her, but each time Cyndi moved to block him.

"You can try to avoid me, but it isn't going to work," Cyndi stubbornly declared. "I'm going to follow you until you tell me about your training."

After trying his best to evade her, Lance stopped. "No, Captain Stafford, you won't."

"Wanna bet?" Cyndi defiantly crossed her arms, blocking his path.

Lance chuckled. "Twenty bucks says you won't keep following me."

"You're on. Twenty bucks it is."

He pointed above her head. "Read the sign." When she turned to look, he slipped past her and went into the men's locker room.

———◆———

General McNeil stormed into his office and immediately bumped into a step ladder.

Oliver Higgs, a scrawny, pimple-face nerd, clutched the wobbly ladder with one hand while he secured the cover to a smoke detector. "Hey, watch it, asshole," he barked, without taking his attention off the cover.

"What the hell did you say?"

When he looked down, Higgs's face paled even more. "Oh, crap." He scrambled down the ladder and fumbled a weak salute with his left hand. "Sorry about that, General, sir. I didn't realize it was you."

McNeil pointed his finger in Higgs face. "Son, you are damn lucky you're a civilian." He looked up at the ceiling. "What the hell are you doing up there?"

"Replacing the battery," he replied with a squeaky voice.

A tiny red light on the cover blinked every five seconds.

McNeil's eyes narrowed. "Didn't you change it last week? And the week before that? Don't you have anything better to do?"

"Leave him alone, General. It needed a new battery." Lola Crawford, executive secretary to General McNeil, had no hesitation coming to the defense of the frightened nerd. Crawford wore skintight leopard-print leggings, huge hoop earrings, and way too much three-dollar perfume.

At twenty-six, she was the youngest executive secretary on the base. Other secretaries had pointed opinions about how she managed to climb the ladder so quickly but only shared them behind Crawford's back.

She wasn't pinup calendar material but was considered the hottest woman in her trailer park by her male neighbors.

"He came over right away when I called. Oliver is like my own personal IT department. He put in a new battery *and* fixed my laptop. He's a friggin' genius with all that tech stuff."

Higgs blushed at the compliment.

McNeil had a perplexed expression as he looked back and forth between the two. Then he burst out laughing. "Kid, she is so far out of your league, it's embarrassing. Take your schoolboy crush and go find a Star Wars convention." McNeil opened the door to his office and pointed to the hallway. "You can get all dressed up and pretend to be somebody."

Higgs folded up his ladder and skulked out of the office with his tail between his legs.

Crawford shook her head in disgust. "You're such an ass."

McNeil planted his fists on her desk and leaned toward her in a threatening manner. "You're speaking to an Air Force general, Miss Crawford. I won't tolerate that kind of insubordination from you or anyone else. You will address me as sir or general."

"Then why don't you fire me?" She tried to goad him with her defiant response.

Surprisingly, McNeil took a breath before pouncing on her blatantly insolent remark. He chose his words carefully. "We both know I can't fire you so soon. Even though your complaint was tossed out, some people might view that as retaliation."

She glared at McNeil. "And some people might say you lied through your teeth."

A self-assured look crossed his face. "Without any evidence to back up your accusation, it wasn't very bright of you to think they'd take the word of a secretary over a one-star. You have a lot to learn about how the military justice system really works. Next time you—"

Colonel Wilmer unexpectedly walked in, holding a manila folder. Sensing the tension in the room, he retreated and said, "I'm sorry, should I come back later?"

"No, Colonel, stay." McNeil straightened up. "I was just explaining something to my secretary that she's confused about." In an offhanded voice he asked, "So, did you remember to send the quarterly staffing reports to the Pentagon, Miss Crawford?"

"Yes, *sir.* Oliver showed me how to save backup copies in the cloud in case I ever need them in the future."

"I'm surprised *you* thought of that," McNeil said in the most demeaning tone he could muster.

"I'm smarter than you think, General," Crawford shot back.

McNeil walked away and waved Wilmer toward his private office. Over his shoulder he got in a parting shot loud enough for everyone to hear. "I doubt that."

Crawford's face turned crimson at the mean-spirited jab. She gave the general the bird behind his back.

McNeil's large private office was a far cry from the spartan outer office. Dark wood paneling covered the walls. Tastefully upholstered couches, an antique coffee table, and overstuffed chairs provided a separate sitting area in front of a roaring fireplace. Pictures of McNeil standing next to prominent people adorned the walls. A door on the right side of the office led to a private bathroom and shower. A massive, carved oak desk dominated the center of the impressive space.

Noticeably absent from the desk were any pictures of family.

McNeil tossed his gym bag on a couch then sat in the high-back leather chair behind his desk. The large chair looked as if it could swallow him whole.

Colonel Wilmer stepped forward, stood at attention,

and began his report. "Sir, I have determined what—"

McNeil held up a hand, stopping the colonel in mid-sentence. He lifted the lid on an ornately carved wooden box and pulled out a Winston Churchill-size Cohiba Esplendido. McNeil had a friend in Washington smuggle the expensive cigars into the States in a diplomatic pouch. He meticulously trimmed the end then lit it with a gold-plated lighter. Without saying a word, he waved for Wilmer to continue.

"Yes, sir. As I was saying, I've determined what happened this morning."

McNeil leaned forward and pounded his fist on his desk. "Someone is going to hang because of this screwup, and it sure as hell isn't going to be me."

"Of course not, sir. This regrettable incident happened because Master Sergeant Holmes failed to check the SD card before he inserted it into the computer."

McNeil cocked his head. "So, you're saying it's your NCOIC's fault?"

"Absolutely, sir. It's inexcusable he wouldn't have checked the card first."

After deftly navigating the cutthroat world of military promotions for decades, McNeil knew exactly what was motivating Wilmer's explanation. "What do you recommend I do about this, Colonel?"

"I would never presume to think that I would have a better solution than you, sir." He stared at his shoes and shifted his feet. "The thing is…"

"Spit it out, Wilmer."

"I'm afraid anything less than a court-martial would send a dangerous message to your troops, sir." He looked up. "They might wrongly assume you are weak. It's not true, of course, but you know how quickly groundless rumors can spread on social media these days—and at the officers' club."

McNeil leaned back in his chair and took a deep draw

from his smuggled cigar. He let it out slowly. The acrid smoke curled up toward the ceiling like a poisonous snake. "Have the paperwork ready for my signature by the end of business today."

Relief washed over Wilmer's face as he exhaled. "I took the liberty of preparing the legal paperwork before I came over, sir." He opened the folder. "It's ready for your signature."

"How efficient of you," the general said derisively. He snatched the folder out of Wilmer's hand, opened it, and scribbled his signature on the document. McNeil waved away the backstabbing Wilmer. "Now get the hell out of my sight."

He scampered off before the general could have a change of heart.

With the simple stroke of a pen, the exemplary career of Master Sgt. Mark Holmes had been destroyed.

The intercom box on the desk buzzed. Lola's irritating voice crackled over the small, cheap speaker. "General, your boss is on line two."

McNeil sat up straight in his chair and flipped a switch on the box. "Did he say why he was calling?"

"Yeah, he did." The sound of gum chewing overlaid her response.

"Well…?" McNeil shot back with exasperation at her attempt to play games.

"He wants to know your favorite color."

McNeil hit the switch on the intercom so hard he broke it off. He took a few deep breaths to calm himself then picked up his phone. "General Rayburn, I was expecting your call."

"What the *hell* is going on at your base, McNeil!"

His rebuke was so loud, McNeil had to pull the receiver away from his ear a few inches to prevent hearing damage.

"I just got off the phone with the president. The friggin' *commander in chief*! He ordered me to come to the White House first thing tomorrow morning with a full explanation. I sent you to Cheyenne to clean up that mess, not nuke North Korea!"

"Yes, sir. I understand, sir. You're completely justified in being angry. I've done a thorough investigation and was shocked myself at the incompetence on display this morning. The command post NCOIC is the man responsible for this fiasco. I assure you; it's not going to go unpunished."

"You're damn right about that!"

"I just signed the paperwork authorizing a court-martial for him. I will forward it, and a complete explanation of what happened to you by this afternoon, sir."

General Rayburn hadn't gotten to the rank of four-star general without learning how to play the blame game. He needed a high-ranking scalp to show his boss. "It's too late to dump your ass now, McNeil. The rollout of the new Minuteman IV at Warren is just three months away. But once the weapons system is up and running, the Air Force will no longer be needing your services."

Rayburn slammed his phone down.

General McNeil had just learned the harsh lesson that knives cut both ways.

# CHAPTER 8

CYNDI ROLLED INTO the dark parking lot of the badly misnamed Front Range Riviera apartment complex. Daylight savings time had ended a few weeks ago, and the long, frigid nights had begun.

She pulled her silver Honda Accord into a spot in front of her building and tossed her go-bag into the back seat. Dressed in civilian clothes again, the young woman—responsible for commanding the most devastating weapons the world has ever known—looked like any other local. Cyndi flipped the hood of her parka up and gathered the four plastic grocery bags sitting on the front seat. When she opened her car door, the incessant Wyoming wind tore the handle out of Cyndi's hand. The only thing that prevented the wind from ripping the door off its hinges was the side of the car next to her. Dings from wind-blown car doors were so common in Wyoming that drivers didn't even bother leaving a note. Cyndi hefted the grocery bags out of the car and headed up the sidewalk.

Across the parking lot, two ranch hands wearing faded jean jackets and muddy Red Wing boots lurked in the cab of a rusted F-150. The driver, sporting a mullet under his oil-stained baseball cap, tossed an empty beer can out his window. His passenger propped the plaster cast covering his right arm on the window ledge and tipped his cowboy hat down over his eyes.

The driver caught sight of Cyndi as she headed for the

building. He slapped his buddy across the arm. "There's our next six-pack, Billy. Let's go."

The men quietly slipped out of the truck and moved quickly toward Cyndi from behind.

Mullet Man pulled a switchblade covered with faux pearl out of his back pocket. He pressed a button on the side and flicked open the razor-sharp six-inch blade.

Cyndi struggled with the heavy plastic bags, trying to keep them from splitting open before reaching the building. With the men only ten feet away, she put the bags down on the sidewalk, as if to get a better grip.

"Hand over your wallet, bitch," the driver growled, pointing the knife at the back of Cyndi's neck.

She spun around and kicked the knife out of his hand in one fluid motion. It sailed away into the darkness and buried itself in a snowbank. "Can I help you idiots with something?" she calmly asked the stunned cowboys.

"Oh, it's you, Stafford," the passenger said, his voice quivering. "We didn't mean nothin'. Just messin' around."

Cyndi taunted him as she pointed at the cast on his arm. "You're a slow learner, Billy. I thought you'd be more reluctant to bother me again."

Billy's head drooped as he kicked at the sidewalk.

His buddy gawked at him in disbelief. "You got your ass kicked by a girl? You told me you got bucked off a horse."

Cyndi pointed toward the parking lot. "Why don't you two sod busters be on your way." She pinched her nose. "And next time you're at Walmart, try buying a bar of soap, for God's sake."

They turned and scurried back to their truck.

Cyndi entered her building and knocked on the first door she came to.

An elderly woman wearing slippers and a faded flower-print muumuu answered the door. She opened it as far as the security chain would allow and peered out suspiciously. "Who the heck are you?"

"Hi, Ruby; it's Cyndi. I've got your groceries for the week."

Thick prescription glasses hung from her neck on a silver chain. She hoisted them in place and squinted. A big smile suddenly crossed Ruby's face. "Well, I'll be. Come on in, dearie." She unlatched the chain and ushered Cyndi in.

Once a rough and tough cowgirl in her youth, Ruby was now wafer-thin, stooped over, and needed a cane to walk even the shortest distances. An oxygen canula encircled her head. The plastic feeder tube trailed Ruby wherever she went, occasionally entangling her feet like an overeager puppy.

She hobbled over to the kitchen table, pushed aside a stack of coupons, and told Cyndi, "Put them here."

Cyndi's biceps rejoiced after depositing the heavy bags on the table. She flopped her arms around like wet spaghetti to work out the tension. She'd spared no expense getting the best options the local Safeway had on its shelves. Cyndi reached in and pulled out a bounty of healthy, nutritious food from the bags. She put each item away in its proper place.

"Did you get the chocolate cake Henry likes so much?" Ruby asked. "I nag him all the time about how bad it is for him, but he don't listen. Mule-headed fool."

Cyndi laid a hand on Ruby's shoulder. "Henry has been gone for over a year now. Remember?"

Profound sadness washed over her weathered and wrinkled face. "Oh goodness gracious. My darn memory is shot to hell. Gets worse every day. Doc Worthington says there's nothing more he can do. Says one day I won't even be able to remember my own name." She looked at Cyndi with a weary expression. "Don't go gettin' old, dearie. Nothing but problems."

Being defenseless against the cruel toll aging took on

her body and mind were all too familiar realities to the once strong woman.

Cyndi changed the subject. "Do you have the coupons for next week?"

Ruby gathered up seventy-five cents' worth of coupons and handed them to Cyndi. "You wipe out all those dang commies yet?"

"No, not yet. Maybe tomorrow, Ruby."

"You better hurry. We got so many damned missile silos in these parts it looks like an outbreak of chickenpox on a map. We'd be nothing but a glowin' hole in the ground if they ever decided to kick off World War III."

"I'll see what I can do."

Ruby cocked her head and looked into Cyndi's tired eyes. "You okay, dear? How was work today?"

"Very strange."

"Did I ever tell you I worked in the Powder River coal mines when I was your age?"

"I think you might have mentioned it once or twice," Cyndi said with a patient voice and an understanding smile on her face.

"That was some tough work. I worked twice as hard as the guys just to get half the pay. Even then, they told me I was stealing a job from the men in town who were trying to feed their families. But I laid down the law with the fellas on my first day. I told them, 'I was raised on a farm with five older brothers, so I ain't about to take any guff from you damned rednecks.' They got the message real quick. If any of those boys out at the base give you any trouble, you send them over my way. I'll fix their wagon, but good. Us girls, we have to stick together."

"Thanks for having my back, Ruby. I'll remember that."

The old woman plucked a handful of tattered one-dollar bills out of her pocketbook. "How much do I owe you?"

Cyndi reached into the last grocery bag, crumpled up

the receipt, and quietly slipped it into her pocket. "You already paid me for the groceries when I came in. Don't you remember?"

Ruby bounced the heel of her hand off her wrinkled forehead. "My darn memory is shot to hell. Gets worse every day. Doc Worthington says there's nothing—"

"Okay, Ruby, have a nice night. I'll come by tomorrow to check up on you." Cyndi let herself out before the entire conversation with Ruby could be replayed. She went across the hall and unlocked the door to her apartment. When she opened it, an object darted toward her.

A fluffy black-and-tan Yorkshire Terrier ran up, bouncing up and down like an over-caffeinated four-year-old.

"Silo!" Cyndi shouted with equal excitement. "How are you, girl? I missed you." She scooped up her dog and gave her a big hug. Silo began furiously licking Cyndi's face when she headed toward a certain cabinet in the kitchen. She opened the cabinet door and grabbed a bag of Purina, pouring out a small helping in the dog bowl. "Bon appétit." Silo dove in before the bowl even hit the floor. Cyndi dumped out the old water from the second bowl and refilled it.

After Silo was taken care of, Cyndi pulled a frozen enchilada dinner from the freezer and popped it into the microwave. When the timer went off, she pulled the steaming meal out and gingerly transferred it to her kitchen table as quickly as possible before burning her fingers.

Cyndi stabbed at the unappetizing blob of Mexican food while she watched a young anchor with KGWN read the evening news. The lead story was about the city council approving the budget for an additional snow-plow. Big news in a small town.

After taking a few bites, she pushed the tray away. She looked around her small, sparsely furnished apartment. On a coffee table were wooden models of an Apache helicopter and an F-35 Lightning II. Next to them was a faded picture of her father posing on the boarding ladder of an F-15 Eagle. In the photo he was clutching his flight helmet under his arm. His confident pose exuded his usual fighter pilot swagger.

There was no question she was her father's daughter. From her steel trap of a mind to an ego she had to work to keep in check, Cyndi was most definitely Brock "Razor" Stafford's daughter. Even the resemblance was striking. Cyndi dwelled on the picture for a moment then let out a heavy sigh. A single tear trickled down her ivory cheek. She got up and tossed her dinner in the trash.

Cyndi marched off to her bedroom, emerging a few minutes later wearing baggy gray sweatpants emblazoned with large block letters spelling out USAF. A tight white spandex tank top, pink Nikes, and black fingerless exercise gloves rounded out her outfit.

Cyndi stormed into the modest workout room in the basement of her apartment complex. She jumped on the stationary bicycle and cranked the resistance up to the max. After ten grueling miles, she did a set of twenty reps at each station of the weight machine. Next, she attacked the heavy bag hanging from a chain attached to the ceiling. It was the size of a water heater and covered in faded, peeling leather. She unleashed devastating kicks and punches on the hapless bag, splitting open duct tape that had held together a previous split.

Ten minutes later, she slumped down to the floor and leaned against the wall, drenched in sweat. Cheyenne was almost one thousand feet higher in elevation than Denver. The thin air left her lightheaded and gasping for oxygen. Cyndi closed her eyes and forced herself to moderate her breathing. Once it had returned to normal, she stood up and gave the bag one more powerful roundhouse kick for good measure.

Back in her apartment, she cranked up the temperature in the shower as hot as she could stand it. Slowly, the steam bath washed away the tension in her muscles. Sweat and Wyoming dust were swept away by the soothing spray. But no matter how hot she got the water or how many gallons she wasted, the guilt that haunted her refused to drain away.

Cyndi gave up and got ready for bed. She changed into a T-shirt adorned with a rendering of Pistol Pete, the U of W mascot. She'd snatched it out of the air at a basketball game when it was shot into the stands from an air cannon.

She nestled under a thick, down-filled blanket and flipped open a thriller novel by her favorite author. Silo lay curled up at the foot of the bed.

Just as she began to drift off, her iPhone rang. She rolled over and looked at the Caller ID on the screen. "Oh crap."

# CHAPTER 9

S HE TAPPED THE screen. "Hello."

"Hi, pumpkin. It's your mother calling. I'm still alive in case you're wondering."

"I'm so sorry. I meant to call you back."

"You scared the daylights out of me."

"I didn't know it was a false alarm when I called you this morning. We only learned that later. It's been crazy all day. They locked down the base. No phone calls were allowed in or out after that."

Silo got up, extended her front legs, and arched her back. She came over and snuggled up next to Cyndi.

"Don't worry about me. I'll be okay," her mother said in a passive-aggressive tone Cyndi had heard many times before. "Your tour in the *missile command,*" she said the words as if they were the name of some awful disease, "will be over soon. I know we've talked about it before, but…"

"Mom, don't start with that again."

"You'd be perfect for the job. What else would you do when you get out? I can't imagine there's a huge demand in the business world for employees who specialize in vaporizing the competition."

"My job is called missile combat crew commander. And there's a lot more to it than just that. Besides, I'm not interested in taking over Dad's job running the flight school now that he's gone."

"Business is really booming. I could sure use the help."

"Sell it then. Move to Florida. Enjoy life."

"I couldn't do that. You know me, always have to stay busy."

"Get Stevie to help out then. He certainly has the time."

"Oh no, I couldn't ask your brother to help. You know how stress upsets him."

"No, we wouldn't want to upset poor Stevie." Cyndi took a calming breath. "When I get out, maybe I'll look for a job here."

"Wyoming?"

"It's not so bad. There's a sort of rugged, untamed vibe here. It's like stepping back in time. People look you in the eye when they talk to you. I can breathe the air without coughing. No police helicopters flying over the house every night. No traffic jams. Unless you count a herd of antelope crossing the road and blocking traffic."

"Animals running loose in the city? That sounds positively dreadful."

Silo growled at hearing her last comment.

"Far be it for me to say anything, but…" Her mother left the unfinished sentence hanging in the air.

"Yes, Mother, what is it? I know that tone," Cyndi said, exhaling loudly.

"Anything new in the boyfriend department?"

Cyndi held her phone up to her face and silently screamed at the screen. Once she'd gotten that out of her system, she said, "You just don't let up, do you, Mom?"

"I just don't understand how a beautiful girl like you doesn't have boys lined up outside your door. That's all. So sue me."

Cyndi got out of bed and wandered into the kitchen with the phone cradled against her shoulder and cheek. She pulled a quart of Rocky Road out of the freezer, then grabbed a spoon. "Maybe it's the job. Civilians don't understand why I do it, and the guys at work are intimidated by me. As soon as I want to get serious, they suddenly get spooked. What is it with men? They act like being in a committed relationship is worse than standing on a pile of radioactive kryptonite that's on fire. Guys can be so infuriating."

Cyndi refused to believe that her hard-earned success in the martial arts could have contributed to her dismal track record with guys.

From her first lesson as a young girl, her parents had taken decidedly different views on her involvement in the violent sport.

Cyndi's dad had pushed her every step of the way as she climbed the national rankings. He never missed a match no matter how far he had to drive.

Her brother had never shown any interest in sports. Looking back, Cyndi couldn't help but wonder if her father's obsession with her winning was more about soothing his disappointment in Stevie than taking pride in her accomplishments.

Her mother had refused to attend her matches. She felt it wasn't ladylike for a girl to wrestle around in a smelly gymnasium with a bunch of sweaty boys. In high school her mother had made her opinions crystal clear. She told Cyndi no teenage boy wanted to be teased about how their girlfriend could put them in the hospital if he crossed the line with her. Their fragile egos wouldn't allow it.

So much for equality among the sexes.

"You do what's best for you, pumpkin. I don't want to make you feel guilty."

"It's a little late for that." Cyndi plunked down at the table and scooped out a big helping of frozen solace.

# CHAPTER 10

*One month later*

CYNDI PULLED OUT of the parking lot of the Front Range Riviera apartment complex to begin her morning commute. The drive was a delightfully short five minutes—a far cry from the snarled nightmare that is Los Angeles traffic.

Every driver passing the opposite way gave a friendly wave of the hand, as was the custom among locals. It had taken her a while to get used to this practice. A motorist in LA shaking their hand at you had a completely different meaning than here in Cheyenne.

Cyndi turned onto Randall Avenue, the road leading to the main gate at the base. A modest brick sign proudly proclaimed that Warren AFB was the Home of the Missileer. She got in line behind four cars waiting to enter. As she inched along, she looked over at the three massive nuclear missiles on display—an antiquated Minuteman II, a Minuteman III, and a Peacekeeper. The glossy white missiles chronicled the never-ending evolution of technology and destructiveness.

The line of cars moved quickly past the guard house until it was her turn. When the guard caught site of Cyndi, the young airman suddenly decided it was imperative that he leave his warm hut and personally check the picture on her ID against her attractive face. Then he walked around her car and did a slow visual inspection.

The guard handed back her ID, flashed a flirtatious smile, saluted smartly, and wished her a good day.

The parking lot in front of the base theater had filled up fast. Rumor was that a four-star general had flown to Cheyenne and was making a big announcement today. By order of General McNeil, attendance was mandatory for all officers. He didn't want his boss speaking to an empty room. No flight suits were allowed at this event. Air Force blues were the uniform of the day.

Lance Garcia walked into the theater lobby with his buddies. When he turned to enter the auditorium, he accidently bumped into Cyndi. "Sorry about that, Captain Stafford. Didn't mean to knock into you. Please don't throw me to the ground. I promise I'll never do it again."

His friends laughed the way guys laugh at everything their buddies say.

Cyndi ignored them. "I'll spare you the humiliation in front of your friends, but only on one condition."

"How considerate of you. What's your condition?"

"You tell me the truth about your martial arts training. I'm not buying your lame explanation that watching Jackie Chan movies was why you did so well on our first encounter."

Lance let out a long sigh. "You're not going to let it go until I come clean, are you?"

"You're very perceptive, Lieutenant Garcia. With a mind that sharp, I'll bet you're up for early promotion."

"My friends call me Lance." He stuck out his hand in a gesture of friendship.

Cyndi hesitated, then firmly grasped his hand. "You can call me Captain Stafford, Lieutenant."

Without releasing her hand, Lance leaned in and whispered, "You aren't a Russian spy by any chance, are you, *Captain*?"

She just rolled her eyes and yanked her hand away.

"I could have my top-secret security clearance taken

away if I tell you. But…in this one case I might be willing to take that risk." He locked eyes with her and waited.

Cyndi crossed her arms and glared back. "If?"

"You still owe me twenty bucks. But I'd be willing to let that slide if you buy me dinner."

"You want *me* to buy *you* dinner?"

"Or…you could make me dinner. Your choice." A cocky grin spread across his face. "That's the price for divulging my secrets."

She stroked her chin. Cyndi inhaled slowly, then said, "I'll think about it. Although…there is a well-known restaurant in town I think you'd be happy with. It serves your favorite meal."

"My favorite meal?"

"The one that comes with fries and a toy in it." With a triumphant smirk, Cyndi strode off into the auditorium.

The entire front row had been reserved for members of the press. Only three showed up. Two were from the local *Tribune Eagle* newspaper.

The audience snapped to attention when the commander of the Global Strike Command, General Rayburn, walked out onto the stage and took his position in front of the podium. McNeil and a thin, high-strung Asian man trailed behind him.

"Seats," Rayburn said, in a commanding voice.

The crowd sat down. The lights were dimmed.

The movie screen behind the general lit up with the first slide in the PowerPoint presentation. It showed his official Air Force photo, name, and rank. The left breast area of his blue uniform jacket looked like a fruit salad had exploded onto it. Dozens of multicolored service ribbons decorated his jacket, the sign of a broad career and a long tenure in the military.

Then the second slide came up.

A noticeable murmur arose from the crowd of missileers.

The reporters turned and looked back. They were at a loss as to why the crowd was reacting to the slide. To them, it was just a picture of a Minuteman missile, but the experts in the audience knew differently.

The nose cone on the missile was longer and wider.

# CHAPTER 11

"I'M SURE YOU'VE all heard the rumors floating around about a new weapons system," Rayburn said. "I'm at Warren today to end the rumors and announce that your base has been chosen to be the first to deploy the updated LGM-30H Minuteman IV missile."

Heads nodded in approval. Applause broke out among the missileers in the audience.

Rayburn turned on a laser pointer and used the beam to trace a circle around the top of the missile. "The enlarged shroud on the missile will now house ten W87-1 warheads."

A reporter shot up from his seat, hoping to embarrass the four-star. "General, the START treaty with Russia has only allowed one warhead per missile for decades now."

"I was about to discuss that issue, sir," the general countered through gritted teeth. "If you'll allow me to continue without interruption, I'll be happy to take questions after my presentation."

The chastened reporter slouched back down into his seat.

"After decades of repeated violations of the treaty by Russia, President Donovan made the bold decision after taking office to end America's participation in the START treaty." Rayburn looked closely at his wristwatch. "A few minutes ago, the president made that decision public during a speech at the UN. The past year, in preparation for today's announcement, the Air Force has been secretly constructing a new missile silo that is colocated next to its LCC."

The crowd gasped.

Since 1970, nuclear missiles have been located miles from their launch control center in a hub-and-spoke pattern. Each underground launch control center controlled ten missiles. In theory, dispersing the weapons miles from the launch center (and each other) prevented one bomb from taking out everything. Military strategists defended this arrangement by boasting that it required Russia to waste eleven missiles to destroy a flight of Minuteman missiles and their launch center. Since the US policy was to never start a nuclear war, the silo-based ICBM fleet would act as a gigantic nuclear sponge, absorbing hits from Russian warheads that couldn't otherwise be targeted at your town. Farmers and ranchers who lived nearby these silos weren't quite as enthusiastic about the strategy.

"A new era has begun for Global Strike Command," the general said, beaming with pride. "Our ability to deter war with our enemies through overwhelming strength will now be greatly enhanced. By returning to ten multiple independently targetable reentry vehicles per missile, we will be able to drop a thermonuclear warhead on ten separate targets using only one launch. For you folks, that means 135 of the existing silos in this area will no longer be needed. This superior strategy, that I personally crafted, will reduce costs by 90 percent for missiles, maintenance, and manning. Not only that; the refurbished sites housing the new Minuteman IV will also have the latest security technology. The above-ground facility that previously required an entire support team to operate will now be unmanned, autonomous, and self-sufficient. This exciting new paradigm will be called *Alpha*."

Rayburn had come up with the name himself. He was

positive a lower-ranking person could never have come up with such a clever moniker.

The general failed to get the rousing round of applause he was expecting from his grand announcement. Airmen in the audience who provided support at the current missile sites weren't thrilled about being replaced by circuit boards and computer chips.

General McNeil picked up on the lack of enthusiasm. He faced the crowd and clapped vigorously. His troops took the hint. They reluctantly stood, gave Rayburn a polite but subdued round of applause, then plopped back down in their seats.

The impertinent newspaper reporter raised his hand. Without waiting to be called on, he remarked, "Ten MIRVs on one rocket? Really, General Rayburn? With this new arrangement, the missile and its LCC can be wiped out with only one Russian nuke. How is that better?" Before the four-star could answer, the reporter followed up with, "And how about those rockets? They came out the year the Beatles broke up. Are the missiles going to be replaced with something that even remotely resembles modern technology?"

The general did an admirable job reigning in his irritation with the disparagement of his grand plan. He forced a smile and said, "Unfortunately, massive cost overruns in the new B-21 Raider stealth bomber program have forced the planned upgrades to our missiles to be cancelled."

"How about the LCCs?" the reporter shouted out. "The calculator I used in college was more advanced than the computers running the launch control centers today. Any plans to upgrade them, or are you sticking with the baffling strategy you people call security through antiquity?"

The reporter was referring to the unofficial moniker the missile forces had given to the justification for using outdated tech to control the most destructive weapons on the planet. In a perverse twist of logic, computers in the LCC were so old and obsolete they were actually *less* vulnerable to hacking than modern technology. Senior leadership had yet to come up with a better slogan to gloss over the fact that the equipment controlling ICBMs in the US arsenal was notoriously unreliable and prone to failure.

"There's no money in the budget to upgrade LCCs at this time," the general admitted in a rare moment of candor. "But you have my personal assurance they are fully capable of doing the job."

"That's comforting," the snarky reporter replied.

Rayburn quickly redirected the conversation. "I want to introduce the chief scientist in charge of developing the new warheads and targeting system, Dr. Li Jun Zhao."

The thin man next to McNeil bowed respectfully toward the general. A black-and-white photo popped up on the screen showing Dr. Zhao as a young man standing next to his family. Zhao, his beautiful wife, and young daughter beamed with pride in the photo.

"Dr. Zhao was the top scientist at the China Aerospace Science and Technology Corporation—a puppet agency of the military. That was, until his eight-year-old daughter made an innocent joke about the premier of China. The regime's reaction to that inexcusable indiscretion was swift and brutal. He was fired from his job, and his wife and daughter were arrested and imprisoned at the Masanjia labor and reeducation camp. After trying in vain for two years to get information about his family, he learned they had died a year earlier under mysterious circumstances while at the camp."

Dr. Zhao's head slumped at the recounting of his painful past. He pulled out a tattered handkerchief, removed his glasses, and dabbed at his eyes.

"Your commander, General McNeil, was instrumental

in helping Dr. Zhao escape that barbaric country and establish a new life here in Cheyenne. America is truly fortunate to have such a genius working for our side. They have been collaborating on the design of the new hardware in the LCC and Minuteman IV for the last year. I'm proud to announce that on February first, the new weapons system will go live."

Dr. Zhao turned, nodded quickly, then bowed deeply toward McNeil.

McNeil wasn't about to bow down to anyone. He patted the doctor on the back then whispered, "Stand up for Christ's sake."

Rayburn looked back. "General McNeil has informed me he wishes to spend more time with his family and will be retiring once the new site is operational. The Air Force is going to miss him."

The excuse Rayburn had used to explain McNeil's retirement was the same drivel most organizations use when there is a lot more to the story than meets the eye.

Rayburn didn't waste any time dwelling on McNeil's departure. "I haven't had an opportunity to notify his replacement yet, but I'm confident he won't mind if I take this opportunity to let him know. I've decided to nominate Col. Stanley Wilmer to be your new commander. I'm also announcing his promotion to brigadier general." He scanned the crowd then pointed. "Brigadier General-select Stanley Wilmer, please stand up."

Wilmer didn't hear the leader of the Global Strike Command call his name. He was too busy trying to remember the items on the grocery list his wife had given him. Officers around him prompted and pushed him to get out of his seat. He looked around, confusion obvious on his face.

"General Wilmer, if you'd be so kind to stand and be acknowledged." The tone of Rayburn's voice told the room he didn't appreciate being ignored when he spoke.

Wilmer slowly rose and gave an embarrassed wave to the crowd. He hastily sat back down.

General Rayburn moved on. Not one to miss out on a chance to appear politically correct, the general eagerly waved McNeil forward. "I believe you have a special announcement concerning the manning of the new site, General McNeil."

McNeil walked up and halfheartedly shook hands with his soon-to-be ex-boss. He turned and took command of the podium after Rayburn stepped aside. "You missileers will be trained and brought up to speed on the new Minuteman IV by the in-service date of one February. The first updated launch facility will be named Alpha One." He pulled a list out of his jacket pocket. "Today I'm announcing my choice for the first combat crew commander to sit alert at Alpha One when it comes online. Based on the extensive investigation I've done, I narrowed my search down to one highly qualified missileer. This person has a perfect record of scoring one hundred on every readiness test, is a distinguished graduate of the Air Force Weapons School at Nellis, and is the most experienced instructor here at Warren. The first officer to command the new Minuteman IV weapons system will be Capt. Cyndi Stafford."

# CHAPTER 12

CYNDI WAS SHOCKED at being picked. Ever since her run-in with McNeil at the gym, she figured she was on his bad side. She had never expected him to bestow an honor like this on her.

"Captain Stafford, come up to the stage," McNeil said, waving her up to join him.

Cyndi stood and straightened her uniform. Before leaving her apartment, she had double-checked that the hem of her skirt stopped exactly at the middle of her kneecap, per regulations. Cyndi took a quick breath, tried to look calm as she marched up the aisle with all eyes focused on her.

Her colleagues gave Cyndi a less-than-rousing round of applause after not hearing their own names announced for the honor.

A buddy sitting next to Lance poked him in the ribs and whispered, "Well, the Russians are safe now."

Lance looked at him with confusion. "What?"

"They picked a *woman* to be the first commander of the Minuteman IV," his buddy explained. "Even with a GPS and a map, chicks still get lost. Picking Stafford just put the 'miss' in missileer." He elbowed Lance even harder and laughed. "Get it?"

"Get with the program, caveman. It's the twenty-first century."

"Tell that to my wife. Every time I get paired with a woman on alert, she throws a fit. She says, 'I don't want any of those whores locked in a room alone with my husband for twenty-four hours.' I don't get any for a month after that, dude."

Lance shook his head. "You're a jerk."

Cyndi arrived on stage and stood at attention between the two generals. Rayburn looked over and motioned for McNeil to step away. The one-star general grudgingly did as he was told. A photographer snapped a picture of Cyndi and the smiling Rayburn. It showed up on the front page of the base newspaper the next day.

———◆———

A huge expanse of gently rolling high prairies on the northern edge of Warren AFB had been set aside for its cemetery. The long history of the base necessitated plenty of room to bury all its fallen. Clusters of gnarled and twisted crabapple trees dotted the landscape. A bitter wind caused the naked branches to shiver.

Major Pierce threaded his way through rows of perfectly arranged white headstones. At thirty-seven, the Delta Force operator had a weary, battle-hardened face that belied his relatively young age. His chiseled jaw was accompanied by an intense look of anger. The rage in his coal-black eyes wasn't the kind that comes from getting cut off in traffic. These were the unnerving eyes of a highly trained killer.

In keeping with the need to conceal his affiliation with the secretive unit, Pierce wore civilian clothing both on and off duty. His job permitted a level of autonomy that few in the military understood.

He knelt in front of a headstone, removed his glove, and brushed away the snow that had piled up against it. The inscription on the headstone was now visible: *E-6 Daniel J. Johnson, 1989 – 2019. Made the ultimate sacrifice for his country.*

"Hey, Johnson. It's been a while." The hint of a smile

crossed his face. "Man, we really kicked some ass in Peshawar. You should have been there. We..." Pierce paused the retelling of his last mission. He couldn't stop reading the last sentence on the inscription. The longer he knelt at the grave, the more anger churned up inside him. He looked around to be certain he was alone. "The team hasn't forgotten what they did to you. They'll pay. Trust me, they'll pay." He got up, stood at attention, and saluted the headstone. Pierce turned and headed back to his car.

---

Sitting alone in the back of his staff car, General McNeil was already on his second shot of Johnnie Walker. His driver knew from past experiences to keep quiet when his boss was in one of his irascible moods. The dismissive treatment in front of his troops by Rayburn had only served to intensify the loathing McNeil felt for the man. "I'm the one who spent countless nights and weekends getting Alpha One ready to deploy, not that pompous ass!" he muttered. McNeil slammed his glass down on the armrest. Expensive alcohol sloshed onto the floor. "I've dedicated my entire adult life to these people, and now I'm being thrown overboard like a rotten fish." McNeil tossed back the remaining scotch in his glass and reached for the bottle again.

---

Pierce was about to get into his car when he saw the dark blue sedan approaching. He went around to the front of his car and stood at the ready. As the staff car got closer, Pierce caught site of the single star on the front license plate. He turned his back to it. The car sped by without even slowing down.

Pierce started his midnight-black Dodge Charger and cranked up the volume on the local rock station. Despite the subzero temperature, he left the heat off. The major depressed the clutch, shifted into first gear, and stomped on the gas pedal. The 6.4-liter V8 roared as he bolted away from the curb. As he raced by the front gate, his cell phone rang. Pierce looked down at the screen and cussed under his breath. The caller was familiar. Pierce held his phone to his ear. "What do you want?" After listening for a few moments he ended the call by saying, "I'll be there."

———◆———

At exactly 1630 Major Pierce walked into General McNeil's outer office. He wore jeans, hiking boots, and a puffy down-filled winter jacket that made his muscular frame look even bigger and more intimidating. "I'm here to see General McNeil," he announced.

Miss Crawford pecked away at her keyboard with two fingers, typing yet another pointless report. Without bothering to look up, she chomped on her gum and said, "Office hours are over. Come back tomorrow."

Pierce marched over to Crawford and leaned down. Veins in his temples were bulging out. In a frighteningly calm voice, he said, "Bitch, get your boss out here. Now."

Crawford looked up and jerked back in fear. She fumbled with the intercom box and flipped a switch. "Sir, there's someone out here to see you." She moved her chair as far away from the Special Forces operator as she could.

McNeil emerged from his private office. "I figured it would be you, Major Pierce." He flicked his hand. "Go home, Miss Crawford. You're done for today."

Crawford grabbed her purse out of the top drawer then slammed it shut. "Gladly." She couldn't get out of the office and away from Pierce fast enough.

McNeil walked over to his secretary's desk and sat on the edge, trying to project a relaxed, friendly demeanor. "I saw you at the cemetery. Visiting Sergeant Johnson, I presume."

"That's none of your damned business." The Delta operator crossed his arms and glowered at the general.

"Relax, Pierce," McNeil said, trying to dial down the tension in the room. "I feel just as bad as you do about him."

Pierce exploded. "Bullshit! You knew you were sending my team into an ambush. Johnson was like a brother to me. You're the reason he's dead!"

"That's what you signed up for!" McNeil shouted back. "When the US wants to exfiltrate a high-value asset, it calls you people. The intel we got from Dr. Zhao during his debriefings was very disturbing. He told us the Chinese long-range nuclear missile program was quickly closing the gap. Within a year, they'll be able to strike any city in the US."

"And you believed him? He had every reason to exaggerate the threat. They murdered his family."

"Of course I believed him. You would too if you had a damned clue. Losing Johnson was a small price to get that valuable intel."

"Small price? You bastard." Pierce slammed the office door closed then locked it. He grabbed McNeil by the lapels and hauled him up off the desk. With his right hand, he reached around the back of his jacket and pulled out a Glock 19 from his waistband. "I should kill you right here."

McNeil stepped back and slapped Pierce's left hand off his lapel. "Save the naïve act. You knew the risks more than anybody. So did Johnson." McNeil started toward his private office—where he kept a S&W .38 Special snub-nosed revolver in his desk.

Pierce wasn't a team leader for no reason. He cut off McNeil and shoved him backward. "You're not leaving this room."

"Get the hell out of my way, Major!"

Pierce leveled his gun at the general's forehead. "This is for Johnson."

McNeil didn't even blink. He calmly crossed his arms and asked, "You really want revenge?"

# CHAPTER 13

*Two months later*

CYNDI HADN'T SLEPT much the night before—which wasn't hard to understand. Today she was going to be in command of the single most destructive weapon on earth. The equivalent of 9,500,000,000 pounds of TNT were packed into the nose cone of the Minuteman IV—over three hundred times more powerful than the bomb that was dropped on Hiroshima.

Unable to stay asleep until her alarm sounded, she'd gotten up early and spent extra time ensuring her uniform and appearance met strict Air Force regulations for her big day. Grooming standards were so constricting, they almost prevented females from looking like females. The trivial topics of nail polish and cosmetics each merited full paragraphs in the regs, listing in minute detail what was allowed. For women, hair had to be tightly pinned against the head. Being a natural beauty, getting her long blonde hair in conformance with regulations was the most daunting task Cyndi faced while getting ready each morning.

Fortunately, her neighbor Ruby loved dogs and gladly volunteered to watch Silo when Cyndi was away. Her only worry was that Ruby would forget to feed Silo.

She parked her Honda Accord in the first row and entered the squadron building for the morning briefing. Missile crews beginning their twenty-four-hour alert shift had to first assemble and go over any new intel that might affect their jobs.

Rarely was there anything important to learn that five minutes watching CNN wouldn't have already told them. The briefings just made their already long duty day even longer.

Once she was out of the cold Wyoming air, Cyndi removed her bulky, olive-green parka. Despite the overbearing uniform rules, it was impossible to fully conceal her athletic, shapely body under her tight-fitting flight suit. Fashion models around the world toiled for hours in the gym hoping to achieve a body like hers.

Two stone-faced security policemen stood guard outside the briefing room. They each wore the distinctive navy-blue Security Forces beret. A sign on the door warned that the upcoming briefing was classified.

Lance and a few friends stood outside the room talking. "What did I miss last night?" he asked.

"It was epic, dude," one friend replied. "We went to Lollipops." He pointed at a buddy. "Thompson fell in love. He ended up taking the stripper home."

"I'm sure that will last," Lance replied, heavy on the sarcasm.

"Why'd you ditch us again?" his friend asked.

"Sorry, guys. I was busy."

"What could possibly be more important than—"

"Well, there was the library. Then church. Then helping little old ladies—"

"Very funny. Next time, no excuses."

"Okay, next time for sure," Lance promised.

Cyndi spotted the group and tried to slip by unnoticed. Not surprisingly, the young men noticed her.

One of the missileers had a sling on his right arm. He reached up with his left hand and straightened his hair. "Morning, Captain Stafford. How's it going?"

The others checked their appearances as well.

Cyndi walked up to the man who'd greeted her. "How's the shoulder, Lieutenant? I might have gotten a little carried away during class last week. Hopefully, you learned a valuable lesson, though." She strutted off with a smirk on her face.

The group elbowed each other and snickered. The stone-faced guards couldn't help themselves. They burst out laughing as well.

Obviously humiliated, the officer marched up to one of the guards and said, "Ever heard of shoe polish? Your boots look like shit." He stomped off into the briefing room.

The doors were closed and locked. The long duty period for the next guardians of America's ICBMs had begun.

# CHAPTER 14

A IRMAN 1ST CLASS Lynette Brown, admin secretary for the 322nd Missile Squadron Commander, stepped up to the podium. Not yet of legal drinking age and barely able to see over the top of the podium, the petite woman from Alabama wasn't shy or meek. "Ya'll hush," she barked. "Can't ya see I'm starting the briefing?"

The room full of higher-ranking officers immediately obeyed. Staying on the good side of the boss's favorite was always a good idea, military or not.

"Alert shifts start at noon. Let's get the preliminaries out of the way before you folks post out. No cell phones, cameras, or any other type of recording devices are allowed in the LCC. Store them in your locker before leaving the building. Raise your hand if you meet any of the following disqualifications to sit alert: consumed any alcohol in past twelve hours…"

The guys who'd visited the strip joint the night before slouched down a little lower in their chairs.

"Or if you have taken any medications that could impair your judgement, been under extreme stress from events in your life, or had any unreported interactions with a foreign national in the last month." She looked expectantly at the group.

Rightly concerned about the possible negative impacts on their careers, no missileers raised their hand.

Brown shook her head in disbelief. "Who knew we

had a bunch of saints in the 322nd."

Nervous laughter came from the audience.

"The snowstorm last night dumped two feet of snow in the area, so alert crews will be helicoptering out to their LCCs until county crews can get the back roads plowed. According to the weather office, there is another system headed this way, so don't be surprised if your alert tour gets extended by a day or two."

Groans came from the overworked missile crews. Their homelives were already strained enough as it was by the unyielding demands of the job.

"Crew pairings and the launch facility you're assigned to are on the board." Brown picked up a stack of red envelopes. "Entry authorization codes for each site are here on the podium. Pick up yours before heading out. Lieutenant Garcia, you are backup today in case we need you."

Lance smiled and gave Airman Brown a thumbs-up. Being chained to his phone for the next twenty-four hours certainly beat sitting sixty feet underground in a claustrophobic concrete capsule.

"Sir, the room is yours." Airman Brown stepped away.

Squadron Commander Lt. Colonel Matthew Stone took the podium. The stern expression on the veteran missileer's face and his penetrating stare made him look like a direct descendant of General George S. Patton. The barrel-chested man always wore a freshly starched and pressed uniform. The crease in his pants was as sharp as his tongue. Times being what they were, he refrained from slapping subordinates who infuriated him. A good tongue lashing was always an option though.

"You sorry bunch of misfits are about to be responsible for this country's nuclear arsenal, so listen up. Nothing less than perfection is tolerated in Global Strike Command. There's too much riding on it to accept anything less. The amount of responsibility Uncle Sam entrusts in you is unlike anything your friends back home will ever see. They can sleep because we never do. We have the most difficult job in the Air Force—constantly being ready and willing to deploy a weapon nobody wants to use. But in the dangerous world we live in, our country doesn't have a choice. Good people must be willing to fight in order to live in peace. Always been that way. Always will be."

With the sermon over, Stone motioned toward the screen. "First slide."

Video footage of the president of Iran screaming threats to the Great Satan flashed up on the screen.

"On the intel front, the Iranians are causing trouble again in the Persian Gulf. The Navy will be shadowing oil tankers in the Gulf for the foreseeable future to ensure safe passage."

The next slide came up. It was a photo of the Korean DMZ.

"North Korea has gone radio silent ever since we came within minutes of vaporizing their pitiful little country a few months back. Let that fiasco be a lesson to you." He banged the tip of his finger into the podium and glared at the missileers. "That happened because those clowns in the command post failed to do their jobs right. Perfection is the standard in this command. No errors, no mistakes, no exceptions." Stone took a breath then gestured toward the screen. "Next."

A picture popped up of three people dressed in clown suits holding signs.

"Speaking of clowns, the Clowns for Christ peace activists are protesting again today at launch facility Lima One. Don't interact with them when you pass through the gate. Let the security team deal with any members of the group who try to gain access to the grounds."

The next picture on the screen was of Cyndi.

"Captain Stafford, stand up," Stone said.

She slowly stood up, unsure why the commander had singled her out.

A pleased look appeared on Stone's face—a rarity for the man. "The new Alpha One site goes live at noon today. Dr. Zhao is there now finishing the programming to bring the weapons system online. Captain Stafford spent the last two months diligently working with him to help write the updated alert procedures manual missileers will be using for the combined sites. Some of you jokers in this room would do well to imitate her dedication as an instructor." He gave her the okay sign. "Sierra Hotel job, Stafford."

"Um…thank you, sir." Embarrassed at being singled out, Cyndi quickly sat down.

Instead of making her look good, his remarks only served to increase the jealousy toward her among the crews.

The next picture on the screen was of Lieutenant Miller, a missileer in the crowd.

"Miller, stand up."

He did as instructed.

"Since this is your LFA, you have the honor of being assigned Captain Stafford's deputy at Alpha One. In keeping with tradition, since today will be your last"—he fake coughed into his fist rather than say the next word in the three-letter acronym to keep from offending anyone with his language—"alert as a missileer, you get one minute to say goodbye or anything else that's on your mind. Keep it clean. There are ladies in the room."

Lieutenant Miller cleared his throat. "As everyone knows, I'm getting out. All I have to say on my last day sitting alert is…" He reached into his kit bag and pulled out a Budweiser. Miller popped the top and took a big swig. He raised the can and said "So long, suckers. Hello, civilian world." He flipped off the crowd, picked up his bag, and walked out.

Stunned silence filled the room.

Lieutenant Colonel Stone's face turned a bright shade of rage red. He turned to his secretary and stabbed his finger in her direction. "Airman Brown, if you don't *lose* Miller's separation paperwork when it comes to my office, I'm going to book you for a one-way seat on the next Glory Trip. Understood?"

Brown had been in the Global Strike Command long enough to know that being threatened with being strapped to the next test launch of a Minuteman missile at Vandenberg AFB was shorthand for making a career-ending mistake.

"Yes, sir. I'll take care of that," she wisely replied.

Still incensed by the audacity of the lieutenant, Stone turned back to the group. The veins in his neck were throbbing. "Since Miller decided to burn his backup, Lieutenant Garcia, you are now paired with Stafford." He gripped the podium with both hands, leaned forward, and glared at Lance. "I assume you don't have a problem with that, do you, *Lieutenant?*"

Lance sighed but wisely replied, "No, sir." He looked over at Cyndi, shrugged, and gave a small wave.

She didn't wave back.

# CHAPTER 15

STONE FINISHED WITH the same admonition he gave after every briefing. "What missileers have done every minute of every day for decades now has successfully prevented all-out nuclear war with our adversaries. I sure as hell don't intend to have that change on my watch. Do your jobs and do them right. Dismissed."

The missileers quietly gathered their belongings and shuffled toward the door.

Two burly missile protection specialists entered the briefing room.

During transport, dedicated security forces had the critical task of protecting nuclear missiles from terrorists. Guarding silos and launch facilities were also part of their duties.

Dressed for battle, they carried M4 carbine assault rifles, an M9 pistol on their hips, and topped it all off with body armor. Their appearance left no doubt the airmen took their jobs seriously.

"I'm looking for Captain Stafford," the senior-ranking specialist said.

"That's me," Cyndi replied, waving her hand.

He hefted a red metal box about the size of a toaster up onto a table. The box was constructed from hardened steel and had two padlocks on it. The warning, *Entry Restricted to MCC and DMCC On Duty*, was stenciled on its door.

The airman handed a clipboard to Cyndi. "Sign here

to transfer custody."

By signing, she was taking responsibility for the key and launch authentication codes that would send their missile skyward if ordered.

Before signing, Cyndi inspected the box. She looked for any breaches in the welded seams. Then she tugged at the padlocks to verify they were closed. Satisfied everything was in order, Cyndi signed the release form.

The security policeman removed one of the two locks.

Cyndi reached into her camo backpack and pulled out her own padlock. It had four number wheels built into the bottom of the lock body to enter her combination. Cyndi, and only Cyndi, knew the combination. She shielded the lock from view with her body while she opened it. Then she put it on the red box and clicked it shut.

The second airman and Lance went through the same choreographed procedure.

Normally, this process would take place on the red box already in the LCC when the new alert crew arrived to relieve the outgoing crew. With Alpha One going online for the first time today, the box and its classified contents were making the trip with Cyndi.

She put the box in her backpack and zipped it shut.

"I'll get the important stuff," Lance joked. He picked up his backpack and started for the galley to get the food they'd need for their alert tour.

"Lieutenant Garcia!" Airman Brown ran up to him. She acted like a teenage girl with a crush talking to the star quarterback. "Here's your gate entry code for Alpha One." She handed him a red envelope.

"Cool. Thanks."

"This came from the personnel office for you. I wanted to deliver it to you personally." She smiled and handed Lance a white letter-size envelope. "I hope it's good news," Brown said with a wink.

"That was so thoughtful of you. Colonel Stone is lucky to have such a competent and—"

"Hey, Romeo," Cyndi said, as she snapped her fingers, "the helicopter is waiting."

Lance stuffed the envelopes into a pocket on his flight suit and headed off to the galley for the all-important food.

# CHAPTER 16

CYNDI AND LANCE slung their backpacks over their shoulders and walked out onto the base helipad. Each had a 9 mm Beretta pistol strapped to their waist. The two security policemen were right behind them. They'd never let Cyndi out of their sight since transferring custody, under the guise of guarding the red box.

In three corners of the large concrete pad, UH-1N Huey helicopters sat belching smoke as their rotors spun at idle. In the fourth corner, a gleaming new MH-139A Grey Wolf helicopter was just starting its engines. A fleet of the Boeing birds was on order to replace the antique Hueys as the transport helicopter for Global Strike Command.

Being a true Texas gentleman, Lance volunteered to put the heavy backpacks in the cabin. He and the guards climbed aboard the helicopter. It still had that new car smell.

Cyndi looked to the east. A pair of F-16s was in the pattern at nearby Cheyenne airport doing touch-and-gos. She let out a deep sigh and slowly shook her head.

"You coming?" Lance yelled out over the engine noise.

Cyndi looked at him and silently nodded. She climbed in and slid the door closed. Lance grabbed a backpack and handed it to Cyndi. She sat next to him on the bench seat behind the cockpit and placed her pack between her feet. They put on headsets then strapped in. Opposite them sat the guards.

In an intentional display of male chauvinism, the pilot looked back at the lower-ranking Lance and asked, "Where to?"

Before he could answer, Cyndi pressed the microphone button on her headset cord. "Alpha One. Move it."

The copilot programmed a direct course to Alpha One into the flight management computer for the second time that day. Earlier that morning, the crew had flown Dr. Zhao and a guard to the site. With GPS for navigation, the course flown there would be accurate to within three feet—less than the length of the bench Cyndi was sitting on.

A swirling cloud of white snowflakes exploded in every direction as the Grey Wolf lifted off the pad. The pilot turned the craft east and engaged the autopilot.

The frozen Wyoming prairie provided little of interest to look at during the flight. The few ranch houses in the area were spaced miles apart.

Lance tried to make small talk with the guards, but they stayed focused on Cyndi.

He looked out the side window as the helicopter passed to the south of a two-hundred-foot-deep abandoned open-pit mine. The pit resembled an enormous coliseum for giants, complete with tiered bench seating. After fifty million years in the making, it took less than ten years for huge dragline cranes to scoop out the valuable coal. The state had spent years trying to get the small mining company to fulfill its obligation to backfill the pit but gave up after its owner strategically declared bankruptcy.

As the helicopter neared Alpha One, the pilot began his approach. A row of massive lattice-frame steel towers paralleled the road passing in front of the site. Strung between each tower were high-voltage power lines carrying power to rural Wyoming.

The pilot thought it would be hilarious to scare his passengers by coming in high over the towers then dropping straight down onto the helipad. Having checked out in the Grey Wolf barely one week ago, the pilot was still getting used to the new aircraft and was eager to test its capability. Like an elevator headed for the basement, the helicopter began its descent from one thousand feet above the prairie.

The approach suddenly went from a slow drop to a hair-raising plunge.

The four passengers levitated upward in their seats. Lance reached out and snatched the floating backpacks out of the air.

Cyndi turned to the cockpit. "Take it easy, flyboys. I'd rather not see my breakfast again."

She knew they were in trouble when the pilot looked over at his copilot and screamed, "Holy shit!"

He increased power, but counterintuitively, the rate of descent increased. The power increase had churned up the air below the helicopter even more, depriving the blades of smooth air to bite into. In only a few seconds, the helicopter would slam down on the helipad at a speed that wouldn't be survivable. Cyndi mashed the transmit button on her headset cord. "Settling with power! Cyclic forward! Go around!"

The pilot slammed his stick forward.

The descent rate increased even more.

Everyone on board held their breath.

With the ground rushing up to meet them, the helicopter slowly crept forward into undisturbed air. The five massive composite blades dug into the thick, smooth atmosphere. The greater the forward speed, the more control the pilot gained. He pulled hard on the collective to stop the dive. Ten feet from disaster, the descent bottomed out.

Ecstatic at not dying, the pilot let out one more emphatic expletive.

He put the helicopter in a wide, gentle turn back

toward the helipad. The bird set down after executing a mild, cautious approach from the opposite direction.

After the engines were shut down, the pilot turned and sheepishly said, "Thanks, Captain. I owe you one."

Although he tried to hide it, Cyndi noticed his hands were shaking.

# CHAPTER 17

B EFORE LANCE COULD ask any questions, Cyndi slid the door open, grabbed her pack, and jumped out. The guards took up defensive positions on either side of the gate.

Hiding in plain sight was an isolated outpost so dangerous and off limits that deadly force was authorized to keep it secure. The site was the size of a soccer field and encircled by a twelve-foot-tall fence made from reinforced steel. An added deterrent to unlawful entry—spools of razor wire—topped the fence.

Wyoming was a natural choice for nukes. Basing missiles along the northern tier of the US provided the obvious advantage of shortening the flight time over the North Pole to reach cities in our most feared enemy, Russia.

Cyndi opened a box attached to the fence, lifted the handset inside, and said, "Launch control center, this is Captain Stafford at the gate."

A remote-controlled security camera mounted on the fence slowly rotated in her direction.

When it stopped, she heard the guard who had accompanied Dr. Zhao say, "You've reached the wine cellar. State your position, full names, and entry authorization code."

"Wiseass," Cyndi muttered under her breath.

Lance handed Cyndi the red envelope. She opened it and read from the sheet, "Crew commander is Capt. Cynthia Stafford, and my deputy is Lieutenant..." Cyndi paused and pulled the handset away from her ear. She looked down and read the words carefully. Then she looked over at her deputy.

"Yes, that's my full first name," Lance said with an exasperated groan. "What can I say? My mother is French."

"Hey, I'm not judging," Cyndi said, as she fought back a grin. She put the phone back against her head. "My deputy's name is Lancelot Garcia." She thought she heard a snicker coming from the guard. "The entry code is Lima, Seven, X-ray, Zero, Eight, Two, Six. Guards are in place. Requesting entry."

They were put on hold as he verified their information. Bitter cold air seeped through their heavy parkas as they waited. Lance rubbed his hands together trying to generate some warmth.

Two minutes later the words, "Everything checks out," crackled over the handset. "Come on in."

The electronic lock snapped open. The heavy gate squeaked and groaned as it slid across the tracks embedded in the concrete. With the site now vulnerable to attack, the guards raised their rifles and tensed up. As soon as Cyndi and Lance had slipped through the opening in the gate, it stopped and reversed direction. It locked with a heavy, metallic thud.

Twenty yards ahead, a building resembling a mundane ranch house occupied the middle of the grounds. In the past it had accommodated support personnel and their equipment. That had all changed. Now, the building was powered up but empty. Security cameras ringed the property and kept an eye on the site. A two-thousand-gallon diesel fuel tank behind the building fed a generator that backed up the local power supply if it went down. Alpha One was fully autonomous.

Rather than heading for the warm building, Cyndi walked over to a black metal object mounted on a short post. It resembled the combination of a spinning bingo drum and a barbecue grill.

She slipped the paper with the entry code through a slit in the cage, along with the red envelope. Then she pushed a button. With a loud swoosh, flames ignited inside the cage. Seconds later, the classified information was reduced to ashes. Cyndi used a crank handle on the side to rotate the drum. Rocks inside pulverized the ashes, making it impossible to ever piece the remains back together. Lastly, Cyndi scooped out the ashes and tossed them into the air. Strong wind scattered the tiny grains of burned paper across the yard, mixing with billions of other grains.

Consensus among missile crews was that the person who'd devised this cumbersome code-burning routine had watched far too many spy movies.

On the way to the building, they walked by the 110-ton concrete slab covering the silo that protected the missile from the damaging effects of a nearby nuclear blast. Two parallel steel rails led away from the cover. They provided a path for the cover to quickly retract across when it came time to launch.

In case anyone working at the site was uncertain why they were there, stenciled on the silo cover were the words: *MISSILE, NUCLEAR, 475Kt.* On the next line came the glaringly obvious warning—*USE CAUTION.*

An unnerving sound—like the low guttural growl of a predator preparing to strike—emanated from the silo.

Lance put his index finger to his lips as if asking for silence. He gently patted the concrete blast cover as he walked past it. "Down, boy."

At the door to the building, Cyndi waved her military ID in front of a badge scanner. It let out two short beeps. A small hidden door on the wall opened, and a retinal scanner slid out. Cyndi put her face up to it. A vertical beam of green light swept across. The door unlocked and opened.

# CHAPTER 18

CYNDI AND LANCE entered the inconspicu-ous-looking building. The facility that had once bustled with activity now had the eerie ambiance of a haunted house. Cobwebs had formed in the corners of doorways. A layer of dust coated every surface. Stale air greeted every breath.

The interior decorator had apparently graduated from the School of Utilitarian Design. They walked past the TV room where support crews had spent countless hours warding off the monotony. Lance dragged his finger along the dusty vinyl top covering a pool table. Rolled up mattresses sat on rusting metal-frame bunkbeds in sleeping rooms.

An uninitiated visitor would have never known a hard-ened bunker capable of kicking off World War III was buried sixty feet beneath their feet.

Unlike the game of horseshoes, close enough with a ten-megaton Russian nuclear warhead was measured in miles. The building, and its occupants, would have been vaporized by a Russian nuke landing anywhere nearby.

Only a direct hit could destroy the underground bun-ker.

The missile launch officers went to a room in the back of the building and boarded a freight elevator. There were no markings indicating where the elevator led. Cyndi pulled the rusted steel lattice door closed and pushed the only button on the control panel. Thirty seconds later, they stepped out of the elevator.

Fifty years without a sliver of sunlight ever making its way into this subterranean fortress had created a veritable petri dish of nauseating odors. The powerful smell of diesel oil, mold, and dank, stale air assaulted their nostrils. The remaining unidentified odors present would take a team of scientists from a secret government lab to correctly classify.

They were standing in a large, dimly lit area containing machinery that kept the facility operating. A long hallway to the right had various rooms on each side. At the end was a massive steel blast door that looked like a bank vault door on steroids. On the other side was a space so top secret that the public was only allowed to see sanitized, official Air Force pictures of it.

The first ICBMs had gone online back in 1961. The atomic club is so exclusive, more people will get hit by lightning in a single year than the total number of Americans who've ever been missile launch officers.

As they walked toward the blast door Lance ducked into a small room that served as a kitchen to drop off the food.

"Hey, Lancelot, read the sign!" Cyndi called out.

He stuck his head out of the room. "It's *Lance*," he said with a clenched jaw. "Only my mother is allowed to call me that."

She pointed to a sign on the wall. NO-LONE ZONE. TWO-MAN CONCEPT MANDATORY.

The most sacrosanct rule in the long list of regulations designed to protect nuclear weapons was a requirement that no one ever be alone, even temporarily, in any area associated with nukes. The rule eliminated any opportunities for sabotage or an unauthorized launch attempt. By ducking into the kitchen, Lance had momentarily left Cyndi's sight.

"Sorry, my bad." Lance waited for her to join him. He

pulled the box of food out of his backpack, plopped it onto the table, and opened the lid. "Let's see what delicacies we have today."

In the typical missile alert facility, a cook was included in the above-ground staff. Getting hot meals prepared by a talented chef made the difference between a tolerable alert shift and a dismal one. Since Alpha One was fully autonomous, their only sustenance for the next twenty-four hours would come from the cardboard box.

Lance peered down into the box and nodded approvingly. "Nice. T-bone steaks, eggs, bacon, caviar."

"Let me see that." Cyndi nudged Lance aside and dumped out the contents on the table. Bottles of water, bananas, and stale turkey sandwiches wrapped in cellophane tumbled out. "Wonderful," Cyndi said sarcastically. "Just what I was hoping for."

"I'll bet pilots get better food than this," Lance whined.

The official Air Force explanation for the bland, unappetizing food was that it was the polite and considerate menu choice. In other words, it reduced the possibility of farting while sitting next to each other for twenty-four hours in a sealed room.

Cyndi hung her parka on a coat hook, slung her backpack over her shoulder, and said, "Let's go to work."

They approached the blast door. On the outside of it was a painting.

Attempting to bring some levity to the deadly serious job, years ago a crew had engaged in a little gallows humor by painting a mural on the door. Under the rendering of a modified Domino's Pizza box were the words *World-Wide Delivery in 30 Minutes or Less, or Your Next One is Free.*

Cyndi picked up a phone on the wall and said, "It's Captain Stafford at the door."

The four-foot-thick blast door could only be opened from the inside.

Three hydraulic rams the diameter of paint cans slowly forced the massive, sixteen-thousand-pound door open. It took two full minutes.

Cyndi and Lance stepped into a small concrete lined capsule the size of a brown UPS delivery truck.

# CHAPTER 19

THE CRAMPED SPACE was packed with equipment. Computer cabinets lined one wall, and a REACT console was on the other. The updated Rapid Execution and Combat Targeting system console controlled all communication and launch systems. Tubes and transistors had been replaced with microchips and lines of software code. It was the newest piece of equipment in the LCC—installed in 1994.

Curtains hid a single bunk on one end of the space. At the other end was a combination metal sink and toilet commonly found in jails and prisons. With no shower, baby wipes were the only way to freshen up if their alert period was extended. Various human-generated odors had permeated every surface after decades of continuous use. As if the olfactory receptors in a person's nose hadn't been assaulted enough, circuit boards in the electrical equipment gave off a pronounced ozone smell.

If prisoners in America had been subjected to these conditions, ACLU lawyers would be stampeding to the courthouse to file lawsuits.

Visibly upset, Dr. Zhao scampered up to Cyndi. "How you people spend twenty-four hours locked in this dungeon?" Considering the short amount of time he'd been in the US, his English had come a long way. "I only been down here for a few hours, and I have two panic attacks."

"That's right, he did," the guard who'd accompanied the doctor volunteered.

"It's not for everyone," Cyndi answered. "If you're claustrophobic, you are in the wrong business."

"Is everything ready, doctor?" Lance asked as he entered the LCC.

"I do everything I came to do," Zhao sternly replied. He stood at attention in front of Cyndi and saluted. "God bless America. China, go to hell."

Cyndi wasn't sure how to respond to the odd statement. So she returned the salute.

Zhao gathered his things and rushed down the hallway toward the elevator that would take him back up to fresh air and the wide-open Wyoming prairie. The guard grabbed his rifle and sprinted after Zhao to keep from losing sight of him.

"Casa, sweet casa—again," Lance joked as he sat down in the right seat at the control console.

"I expect you to take this alert tour seriously, Lieutenant. I want everything done by the book." Cyndi took the left seat.

Lance turned his head away and mumbled, "Well, you wrote it, so…"

"Close the blast door."

"Yes, ma'am." Lance lifted a red cover on the console and flipped the switch.

Silver hydraulic rams tugged on the massive door. It closed with a resounding thud. Rubber seals inflated around the perimeter of the door, blocking any outside air from entering. Pumps under the floor kicked in, creating positive pressure inside the LCC. The crew was now protected from a chemical weapons attack.

Cyndi and Lance took off their holsters and stowed them in a large storage cabinet under the console.

A monitor on the wall showed Dr. Zhao and the guard making their way across the grounds toward the gate.

The guard opened the box attached to the fence, pulled out the handset, and announced, "Security in place. Open the gate."

Lance looked over at his missile combat crew commander.

"Cleared to open," Cyndi responded.

Lance pushed down the button that controlled the gate. As soon as the doctor and guard were clear of it, he lifted his finger. The gate latched securely closed.

Eager to finish his day and see his four kids, the pilot had already started the engines on the helicopter when he saw his passengers come out of the building.

As the men walked toward the helicopter, they became lost and disoriented. The spinning rotors had kicked up loose snow, causing it to swirl around them.

They felt like they were trapped in an enormous snow globe.

The men made their way toward the helicopter by focusing on the sound of the engines. Out of an instinct for self-preservation, they ducked their heads before walking under the spinning rotors. They climbed aboard, followed by the security detail. Once everyone was buckled in, the helicopter lifted off and took up a course directly back to Warren.

Fifteen minutes into the flight they flew by the open pit mine. After the Grey Wolf helicopter had passed, a pair of black AH-6M Little Bird attack helicopters rose from deep within the pit.

Two FIM-92 Stinger air-to-air missiles hung off the left pylon of the lead ship. Two Hellfire missiles hung from the wingman's ship. Each aircraft sported a GAU-19 Gatling gun on their other pylon.

With no reason to have engaged their defensive systems, the transport helicopter pilots flew toward home, blissfully unaware of the attack helicopters stalking them.

A Stinger missile fell away from the pylon of the lead aircraft. Its solid rocket motor ignited a millisecond later. A white smoke trail blazed toward the unsuspecting Grey

Wolf like Satan's crooked finger.

It homed in on the heat spewing from the exhaust. The warhead detonated the instant it touched the fuselage.

The five men on board shrieked in terror as their dying helicopter corkscrewed down into a deep ravine, miles from the nearest road. It exploded in a blinding orange ball of flames.

The second attack helicopter flew to the ravine and hovered over the twisted, smoldering wreckage. The barrel of its Gatling gun tilted down. A hail of bullets rained down on the charred bodies, guaranteeing there would be no survivors.

# CHAPTER 20

CYNDI TOOK THE sturdy red metal box out of her backpack and slipped it into a slot on the shelf above the launch console. She tossed her backpack into the empty cabinet under the console.

The REACT console had two missileer stations, separated by a large worktable. Duplicate sets of computer monitors, keyboards, switches, and buttons filled the space. A digital clock mounted between the stations counted off every second of every hour, making shifts feel even longer.

Crew members sat eight feet apart in high-back chairs like the ones used by captains on aircraft carriers. The distance between them made it impossible for one person to reach the four most important switches. Those switches controlled more destructive firepower than a hundred floating naval bases.

The effort needed to launch a nuke was minimal. The commander inserted the key from the red box into the designated slot with her right hand. Her left rested on a rotating switch. The deputy controlled two identical rotating switches on his side. On the commander's order, all four would be turned simultaneously. A simple turn of the wrist would unleash 475 kilotons of devastation.

Safeguards built into the system prevented a rogue crew from launching a missile by themselves. Software programmed into the console scrutinized any launch command before executing it by validating it against orders from higher command authorities. If it passed, the missile flew.

"I want everything operating 100 percent before we go to strategic alert status," Cyndi said. "I'll test the communications systems; you run the LCC subsystems test checklist."

"It's only ten o'clock. What's the rush?" Lance asked. "Why don't we eat first?"

"You know the drill. No errors, no mistakes, no exceptions. Your stomach can wait." Cyndi picked up a red phone on her side of the console. "Command post, comm check from site Alpha One." She plugged the opposite ear with her finger, squinted, and leaned forward as she strained to listen. "Say again?" She shook her head. "No. This is site Alpha One, not Echo One." She listened more keenly. "I can't understand a thing you're saying. I'll try the commercial line." Cyndi hung up. "Lowest-bidder piece of junk," she grumbled.

She went over to a wall-mounted phone near the blast door. *Bell Telephone* was stamped on the plastic handset. Cyndi tapped in a phone number on the keypad then waited.

"Warren Air Force Base operator. How can I help you?"

"This is LCC Alpha One. Connect me to the command post."

"Hold, please."

She covered the mouthpiece with her hand and shook her head. "This is ridiculous." After a few seconds she pulled her hand away. "This is Captain Stafford. The direct line at Alpha One is malfunctioning. We are in place. LCC is secure." She listened for a moment then said, "Roger that. And send out a maintenance crew to fix our comm systems." She hung up and sat back down in a huff. "Have you run the checklist yet?"

"On it," Lance said quickly.

He pulled a four-inch-thick binder from the shelf

above his workstation. Every one of the hundreds of pages in the new checklist was tucked into plastic sleeves to protect them from the eventual wear that was to come from being used 24/7/365/forever.

He flipped it open. "LCC subsystems test checklist. Page three dash one one five."

Methodically, he went line-by-line through the checklist with his finger.

"Lamp test." Lance pressed a button. The panel lit up like an overdecorated Christmas tree.

Every switch, button, and bulb on the console would need to be working correctly before the LCC would be deemed fit to control nuclear missiles. Five pages later, he came to the last item on the checklist.

"Backup generator." Lance flipped a switch, but nothing happened. "Come on." He tried it again. Nothing.

"What's the problem?"

"The backup generator isn't responding."

"Try the alternate circuit."

Lance tried a different switch. "Nothing."

"I'm not going to take the site off alert status on its first day." Cyndi got up and walked over behind his chair. She scanned his panel. "Test the generator again."

Lance threw his hands up. "I already did. It's not working."

Cyndi put a hand on his headrest, leaned forward, and pointed. "Try it again."

Lance looked back with frustration. "I've been at this for two years. I think I know what I'm doing, Captain."

Cyndi reached down and pressed the test button herself. Her breasts were now resting on Lance's shoulders.

He tensed up. "I don't think I'm comfortable with this." Lance pushed away from the console and stood up. He turned to face Cyndi.

She straightened up and stepped back. "Is that so, *Lieutenant*? And exactly what are you going to do about it?"

"This!"

Lance cupped his hand around the back of her neck, pulled Cyndi close, and planted a passionate, powerful kiss on her lips.

# CHAPTER 21

CYNDI RECOILED FROM Lance and wiped her lips with the back of her hand. She spread her feet apart to distribute her weight.

Lance swallowed hard, prepared for what was about to come his way.

Instead of knocking him unconscious, Cyndi smiled and said, "What took you so long?"

Lance let out a big sigh of relief. "I wanted to make sure we were all alone. Complete discretion, like you want."

"Now that we are…" She slid down the zipper on her flight suit, revealing a racy, pink Victoria's Secret bra and panties under her military issue uniform.

Lance reached out and slid her flight suit off each shoulder, baring her shapely and toned upper body. He leaned in for a kiss, confident he wouldn't be risking his life this time with his show of affection.

When their lips parted, Cyndi took his hand and led Lance over to the bunk. She pulled the curtains back. "How about we pick up where we left off last night?"

———◆———

Down the hallway in the makeshift kitchen, Cyndi and Lance were eating lunch at a small, faded green Formica table with a dented metal band nailed around the edges.

Cyndi unwrapped her turkey sandwich, put it up to her mouth, then laid it down. She stared down at the table and wondered, *How do I tell him this?* She decided to just be straightforward with how she felt. "The last couple of months have been great."

"The last hour wasn't so bad either," Lance said with a satisfied grin as he polished off his sandwich. He pointed across the table. "You going to eat that?"

Cyndi slid her stale sandwich toward him without answering.

Lance snatched it up and took a big bite.

"You know I care about you—us—right?"

Lance chomped on the sandwich and flashed a thumbs-up. "Ditto."

"It's just that…" Cyndi wavered.

Lance wiped his mouth. He reached out and took Cyndi's hand. "I'm really good at reading women. Something's wrong, isn't it?"

Cyndi nodded.

He took her other hand and looked deeply into her eyes. "You're mad at me for eating your sandwich."

Cyndi yanked her hands away. "Stop kidding around. I'm trying to be serious."

"Sorry. I'll never crack another joke again." He leaned forward and folded his hands. "What's up."

She shook her head. "Forget it. I'm good. Really."

"Talk to me, Goose. Tell me what's bugging you."

Cyndi took a deep breath. "I'm getting out soon, and you still have two years to go."

"About that—"

"I've always known what I wanted in life. Now I'm torn. I'd like to stay in Cheyenne and see where this goes between us, but my mom keeps pressuring me to come home and run the flight school."

"Maybe you should. I know how much you love to fly. I'd hate to be the reason you didn't take the job. If you decide to go back, we could try the long-distance thing. Calls, Zoom chats, text messages."

"That never works out." Cyndi shook her head. "The distance eventually causes couples to drift apart."

"What is it then?"

Cyndi stared down at her hands. "I'm not sure I want to go back to LA. There're too many painful memories back there."

"What do you mean?"

"My dad wasn't the easiest person to get along with. It was always his way or the highway. His favorite saying was, 'If I want your opinion, I'll give it to you.' I'm not saying he was a bad guy. He taught me to fly every plane we had. It's just that he was so damn stubborn. I don't think I ever heard him say he was sorry."

"How did he…you know?"

Her head sagged down. "My mom kept bugging him to go see the doctor, but he said it was nothing. By the time he finally made an appointment, it was too late. The cancer had already spread throughout his body. Regrettably, we weren't on speaking terms back then. He went downhill so fast I never got to say goodbye." A tear trickled down her cheek. She grabbed a napkin and dabbed it away. "I found out later that my bone marrow was a perfect match. I could have saved him."

"You don't know that. There're no silver bullet in medicine."

"At least I could have tried." She looked up with red eyes. "Do you get along with your dad?"

Normally quick with answers, Lance hesitated. "Well… it's kind of complicated. He's always so old school about everything." Lance looked up and tapped his chin. "How can I put this?" He searched for a diplomatic way to describe the challenging relationship between the two. "His idea of parenting was very…traditional." Lance shrugged. "He wasn't around much, though. He's a big-shot heart surgeon in Dallas so he was gone a lot." Hoping to change the subject, Lance slid his chair over next to Cyndi. "Do you know that's the most you've shared about your past since we started dating?"

"It is?" Cyndi said with exaggerated surprise.

"Let me guess. You've been hurt before by guys, so you're scared to open up because it would make you vulnerable." Lance folded his arms across his chest with a great deal of satisfaction. "Am I right?"

"Okay, ease up on the psychobabble there, Dr. Freud. That's not it at all. I'm not scared to show how I feel."

Lance put his hands up. "No, of course not. I completely misread you." He tilted his head. "So, you won't mind if I ask you some questions about your past?"

"Ask me anything," Cyndi responded indignantly.

"Fine. I will," Lance responded in kind.

"Fine."

"I'll start with a hard one. Where did you grow up?"

Cyndi shrugged. "Everywhere. Nowhere in particular. When you're a military brat, you move constantly. No place feels like home."

"That must have been tough. I had it easy. I grew up with the same friends and lived in the same house until I left for the Air Force."

"It affects some kids more than others. Constantly switching schools was the worst part. You'll do almost anything to make friends. Sometimes you hang around the wrong type of people just so you can feel like someone cares about you."

"Can I ask you a personal question?"

Cyndi pulled back. "That depends on how personal it is."

"At the first martial art training class, General McNeil called your dad the 'infamous test pilot.' What did he mean?"

Cyndi checked her wristwatch. "It's almost noon, and the blast door is open. We need to get back to the LCC." She slid her chair back and started to stand.

Lance put his hand on her arm and gently guided her back down into her chair. "We have plenty of time. Talk to me."

She pulled her chair back up to the table. "It wasn't his fault."

"What wasn't?"

Cyndi exhaled deeply. "My dad was testing the YF-24 over the dry lake at Edwards when the plane went out of control. If he hadn't ejected, he would've been killed."

Lance nodded. "I remember reading about that accident. The Air Force said the pilot screwed up."

Cyndi's face suddenly flushed with anger. "That's bull!"

Lance straightened up and lifted his hands. "Hey, I'm just telling you what the Air Force told the press."

"They lied! After I joined the Air Force, I found the accident report. I read every single document in it. A footnote buried in one of the reports said the fly-by-wire software had some bugs in it. I think *that's* why the plane went out of control."

"Did you tell the Air Force what you found?"

"Of course. I called every officer in his chain of command. They refused to talk to me. Said I was reading things into the report that weren't there because he was my dad. When I threatened to go to the press and expose the cover-up, they classified the report. They said the Air Force couldn't risk damaging its relationship with the company that built the plane. Tech Aerospace had just won the multimillion-dollar contract to build the new replacement aircraft for pilot training, and if word got out that their flight software might be unsafe, it would send their stock into a nosedive. I wasn't able to clear his name."

"Damn…that's messed up." Lance grabbed a water bottle from the box and stood up. "I don't blame you for being upset."

"The Air Force refuses to reopen the investigation, but

I haven't given up. One way or the other, I'm going to expose the truth no matter what I have to do." She shook her head. "I don't want to talk about this anymore. All it does is upset me." Cyndi folded her arms and sat back. "What were you going to say?"

He looked away and took a big gulp. Then another one. He slid his chair away from Cyndi and sat back down. He drained the rest of the bottle then cleared his throat.

"Umm…this might not be the best time, but I need to show you something." He pulled out the letter Airman Brown had given him, unfolded it, and handed it to Cyndi.

She read it over carefully. Cyndi folded it up and handed it back. Her head drooped. "That's great," she said softly.

"You could pretend to be a *little* more excited. I've dreamed about being a pilot since I was a kid making model airplanes."

Cyndi looked up and forced a smile. "I'm happy for you. Really, I am."

"You're a terrible liar."

"Okay, you're right. I'm not thrilled. How long before you leave?"

"I start pilot training in four months. I'll be stationed at Laughlin Air Force base. It's in—"

"Del Rio, Texas."

Lance cocked his head. "Have you been there?"

Cyndi got up and walked over to the counter. She turned her back to Lance and rearranged the salt and pepper shakers. She decided the paper plates on the counter needed to be stacked in one pile. Then she split the stack up again. Avoiding eye contact, she quietly said, "Laughlin was my first duty station."

"How could that be? It's a pilot training base. You're a missileer."

She turned and tightly crossed her arms. "We're in the Air Force, remember? Washing out of pilot training isn't something you want the whole world to know about."

"How could someone with your flying experience wash out of pilot training?"

Cyndi plopped back down in her chair. "It's a long story. You don't want to know."

"Try me. Give me the *Reader's Digest* version."

She let out a deep sigh. "Flight school was going great. I was number one in my class. I was only one week away from getting my wings. On assignment night I'd gotten my dream airplane, the F-35. The next day the base commander called me into his office and locked the door. He told me I wasn't going to graduate unless I slept with him."

Lance let out a low whistle. "Obviously, that scumbag didn't know about your martial arts skills, or he never would have tried that with you."

"He found out the hard way when he tried to grab me. I kicked his ass right there in his office."

"Why didn't you report him?"

"A brand-new second lieutenant accusing a lieutenant colonel? With no witnesses? I knew it would be his word against mine."

Lance shook his head. "Hell of a crappy way to welcome you to the Air Force."

"I'd torched a lot of bridges when I challenged the Air Force's official explanation for my dad's crash. The higher-ups were infuriated when I claimed there was a cover-up going on. They were just looking for a reason to kick me out of the service. I wasn't about to hand it to them. So, here I am, a nuclear missile launch officer in lovely Cheyenne, Wyoming." She checked her watch again. "It's noon. Let's talk about this later. We better get back to the LCC." Cyndi stood up.

"Wait." Lance dug into his pocket and placed the object he'd retrieved on the table. It was attached by a short, beaded chain to a rabbit's foot.

Cyndi looked suspiciously at the object as she sat back down. "What's that?"

"The Air Force has a special name for it. It's called a key."

"I can see that. I meant why are you putting a key to your apartment on the table?"

"Before I left this morning, Rocko gave me a slobbery kiss and told me he misses you and wishes you were around more."

"He did?"

"His exact words." Lance crossed his heart.

"Your *dog* told you that?"

"Well…not in so many words. When he looked up at me with those sad brown eyes, I couldn't tell him no. I promised him I'd ask you to move in with us."

"Move in?" Normally very sure of herself when she was calling the shots, Cyndi became flustered at being on the receiving end. She fumbled out a tepid response. "I'm not sure. That's a big step. And you're leaving in four months."

"You don't want to break Rocko's heart, do you?"

"No, of course not."

"It would be perfect. When I'm away on alert, you could take Silo and Rocko to the park for walks. Rocko told me he's tired of the bachelor life. He wants a woman in his life—if only for the next three months."

"What if Silo and Rocko don't end up getting along?" Cyndi said, looking for an excuse to avoid voicing her true feelings. "They're so different. And you know I can't cook."

"Trust me, I know. But I was only in the hospital for two days after you made dinner for me. It's no big deal. We'll order out." He took her hand. "Look, if the Air Force trusts you with the key to unleash Armageddon, I figure I can trust you with the key to my"—a growing blush spread across his handsome face—"my apartment."

"Your...*apartment*. Right." Her twinkling blue eyes smiled. "I'd sure hate to disappoint Rocko. He's much more sensitive than he lets on." Cyndi leaned forward and reached for the key.

Suddenly, the ear-splitting sound of a klaxon blasted out from speakers in the LCC. They bolted up from their chairs, bumping the table.

The key to Lance's apartment tumbled to the floor.

The table toppled over, crushing the rabbit's foot.

# CHAPTER 22

"CLOSE THE BLAST door!" Cyndi yelled as they sprinted into the LCC.

Lance flipped the switch, starting the slow process of sealing themselves off from the outside world.

They grabbed their guns from the cabinet and strapped the holsters around their waists. After years of tedious sessions at the simulator practicing for this very scenario, they didn't hesitate. The missileers went right to work.

Cyndi and Lance strapped in, pulled identical red binders from the shelf above the console, and opened them to the same page in each.

The blaring klaxon abruptly stopped.

They sat, frozen in silence, hoping with every fiber in their bodies that the next sound they heard would be an all-clear message identifying this as a drill.

The sense of tranquility in the LCC was unnerving. They could hear the stale, recycled air gently blowing from the vents.

Time seemed to stand still.

The speaker built into the console suddenly came alive with a five-second-long warble tone. Following the tone, a creepy, computer-generated female voice announced, "This is an Emergency Action Message. Enable code is delta, one, six, November, two, six, foxtrot."

Using grease pencils, Cyndi and Lance wrote the code on plastic-covered sheets in their binders.

"Validate code," Cyndi said.

Lance flipped pages in the binder then meticulously compared the code they'd heard to the one in his book. He looked up wide-eyed. "We just received a valid code."

"That can't be correct." Cyndi read off the characters she had written down.

"It's the same," Lance said after checking her code.

Cyndi stared at the code in her book. "Are you absolutely positive?"

"I checked it twice. It's a match."

She took a deep breath, attempting to get her heart-rate under control. Her foot nervously tapped the floor. "Enter"—Cyndi cleared her throat—"enter the enable code."

"Roger that." Lance carefully typed each character of the code into the computer.

"Enable code entered," the female voice announced.

A vertical row of indicator lights in front of Lance confirmed each step as well.

———◆———

A bright red warning light in the missile silo flashed, accompanied by two loud blasts from a horn. This was the only warning a person working in the silo would have received before being incinerated.

The Minuteman missile came to life as it began its power-up sequence.

Stabilizing brackets supporting the missile retracted.

A plume of white vapor vented overboard and spilled down the side of the missile.

———◆———

POWER-UP SEQUENCE lit up on the next indicator light, indicating the completion of that step.

Cyndi and Lance jumped up and entered their codes in the padlocks attached to the red box.

She opened the box and pulled out an ordinary-looking key. Lance pulled out two cards encased in plastic, nicknamed cookies. They each took one and cracked them open. They both compared the codes on their cards to the earlier code.

The codes were an exact match.

"Upload launch code. Preparatory launch command bravo," Cyndi said.

Lance didn't respond. He couldn't pull his gaze away from his card.

"Lieutenant Garcia, perform the next checklist step. Upload the launch code."

Lance froze. His mind's eye saw a terrifying sight—the inevitable outcome of what they were about to do—the shape of a fiery mushroom cloud.

"Lieutenant!"

Lance looked over. His face was ashen. "The launch code is valid," he said, barely able to force the words past his vocal cords at anything above a whisper.

"I realize that." She repeated her command. "Upload the launch code to the missile. Preparatory launch command is bravo."

Lance typed out the code on his keyboard. His finger hovered over the Enter key. Beads of sweat formed on his brow. He wiped away the perspiration with his sleeve. Then he tapped the key.

---

A thick data transfer cable attached to an umbilical on the side of the missile carried the code to the guidance computer. Once the computer validated the target coordinates, the cable detached and fell away.

Ballistic gas generators detonated, launching massive silo cover door across its rails and through the security fence. Two oval exhaust diverter tunnel outlets and the round opening over the missile were revealed.

The most destructive weapons on earth spent their

pampered lives inside concrete cocoons kept at a pleasant sixty degrees. The silo was now exposed to the frigid winter air.

Ice crystals instantly formed as the different-temperature air molecules collided. Thick fog engulfed the silo, reducing visibility to only a few feet.

———◆———

"Missile ready for launch," the disembodied voice said.

Cyndi inserted her launch key into the console. It slid in effortlessly.

"Slow down; I have a bad feeling about this," Lance said. "Let's take a breath."

"The launch code is valid, Lance. It's our job to execute the launch order."

"I understand that, but…"

Cyndi gripped the head of the key. "Get ready to launch."

"Jesus!" Lance pointed at his monitor. "Our missile is going to take out the ten largest cities in China." His voice cracked. "Over a *billion* people will die if we launch. This…this can't be right. There wasn't a single word about tensions with China in the intel briefing."

"Missile ready for launch," the disembodied female voice repeated.

"It's got to be an exercise, then," Cyndi rationalized. "The president wouldn't just decide to nuke China for no reason."

"But what if it isn't an exercise? Hell, for all we know there could be a bug in the new software. There must be forty million lines of code in the REACT console. Let's get Dr. Zhao back out here and have him check it over."

"I can't. That's not part of the launch procedure. We don't get to decide which launch orders we follow and which ones we don't."

"Dammit, Cyndi, stop quoting regulations. Screw the

manual. What does your gut tell you?"

"It tells me to do my job." She gripped her key even tighter and rested her left hand on her launch switch. "Prepare for key turn," Cyndi commanded.

Lance wiped more sweat from his brow. He reached out and gripped the two launch switches on his side of the console. His damp hands trembled, making holding the switches even more difficult.

"God help us." Cyndi took a deep breath. "Prepare for key turn in five, four, three, two—"

"I can't."

# CHAPTER 23

LANCE PULLED HIS right hand away from the launch switch and shook his head. "I can't do this."

"What are you doing! Put your hand back on your switch."

"Something is wrong about this. It doesn't make sense. Why would we nuke China?"

"What if an attack is underway right now and we did nothing? Millions of Americans will die."

"Why don't we call the command post? They'll know if this is real or not."

"I don't want to start World War III any more than you do, but you know how this works. We don't get to make that decision."

"Missile ready for launch," the female voice repeated over the speaker.

"Put your hand on your switch, Lance. If we don't turn them within two minutes, the missile reverts to standby mode."

Lance ignored her and removed his left hand from the other switch.

"Lance! We're missileers. We have a job to do."

"If you won't do it then I'll make the call." He reached out for the phone on his side of the console.

Click.

Lance looked over at Cyndi. The barrel of her Beretta was pointed directly at his forehead. The safety was off.

———————◆———————

"Colonel Wilmer, you need to see this." Sergeant Morgan, the new command post NCOIC, waved Wilmer over.

He walked up behind Morgan's workstation. "What is it, Sergeant?"

"There's something strange going on out at Alpha One. All communication channels just went down, and the site took itself offline." He looked back wide-eyed. "It's like it just disappeared."

"You've got to be kidding me!" He rubbed the back of his neck and began pacing.

"Shouldn't we call headquarters? Inform the general?"

Wilmer spun around. "No! Wait! Let's not bother him just yet. Run a full set of diagnostics on Alpha One and our equipment. I want to know exactly what's going on before—"

"But sir, that could take an hour to complete."

"Just do it, Sergeant!"

———————◆———————

"What the hell are you doing?" Lance responded with horror.

The gun shook in Cyndi's hand. "I don't want to do this Lance, but I have to."

"No, you don't."

"If China is attacking and we don't launch—"

"If we *do* launch, they will retaliate. Life on this planet is over."

"Lance, please, put your hands back on your launch switches."

He held out his left hand like a stop sign. "I'm going to lift up my phone and call the command post. Don't shoot me." He slowly lifted the handset and held it against his ear. "Command Post, this is Alpha One."

His right arm dropped to his side.

Lance wrapped his hand around the grip of his Beretta and silently pulled it out of the holster.

"Command Post, this is Alpha One. How do you read me?"

"Lieutenant Garcia, I order you to put your hands back on your launch switches."

"Command Post, Alpha One. Do you read me?" Lance slipped his finger inside the trigger guard.

"Lance, please!"

He brought his gun up into view.

"Don't do it!" Cyndi jerked her gun back and forth, aiming at his gun then at Lance. "Put your gun down!"

He hung up the phone in one slow, deliberate move. "The line is dead."

"That could mean we are under attack."

"Think, Cyndi. Take a deep breath and think about this."

"Put the gun down!"

"Okay, I'm putting it down. Relax." Lance took his finger off the trigger and laid the gun down on the worktable between them.

Cyndi kept her gun aimed at Lance.

"This system was built during the Stone Age. What if it just…failed. It wouldn't be the first time." He faced her and looked into her frightened eyes. "There's nobody down here but you and me. We decide what happens next. It's just us. Lance and Cyndi."

"No, no…" She wagged her finger at him. "Don't you say that. Don't you pull that on me."

"Please put the gun down. We can figure this out together."

Cyndi pounded the desk with her free hand. "You have the luxury of second-guessing orders. I don't! I'm the commander. I have a duty to carry out the orders we're given."

"Well then"—Lance let out a resigned sigh—"I guess the ball is in your court, Captain."

The Beretta trembled in her hand.

A battle raged in her heart.

"Lieutenant Garcia, put your hands back on your launch switches."

Lance didn't respond. He turned and stared straight ahead at the console.

"Lance…please, I won't ask you again."

Lance folded his arms across his chest and closed his eyes. Every muscle in his body tensed up.

Cyndi pulled the trigger.

# CHAPTER 24

THE 9 MM slug traveled the five feet between the end of the gun and Lance in milliseconds. It went behind his head and buried itself deep into the mattress on the bunk.

Love had won the battle.

Cyndi holstered her gun, jumped up, and went to Lance. Tears streamed down her face. "I'm so sorry. I couldn't shoot you, no matter what the rules say. I just couldn't do it."

He'd only heard part of what she said because of the loud ringing in his left ear. All he knew was that he was still alive. A huge exhalation of relief left his lungs. Lance stood and embraced Cyndi. "I knew you wouldn't do it. I knew it."

The dangerous world around them disappeared. A prolonged, passionate kiss replaced it.

When their bodies parted, Cyndi hung her head. "I would never hurt you. Can you ever forgive me?"

Lance gently wiped away her tears. "I know that. I don't blame you. You're responsible for the missile. You were just following procedures." He gently lifted her chin. "Next time, maybe just give me a sternly worded reprimand rather than firing a warning shot so close to my head." That irresistible smile he'd used to his advantage many times in the past flashed across his face.

Cyndi fought the urge to be swayed by his beguiling smile. She did chuckle at his poorly timed attempt at humor, though. "Fair enough. I'll warn you next time before I shoot you." She lifted a cover on the console and pressed the button under it. The button lit up. "The missile is in safe mode."

Lance's smile transformed into a look of apprehension. "The missile is safe, but what about our careers? When they find out what we did, there won't be a next time for us."

"You mean *me*. I'm in command. The buck stops with me."

"You did the right thing. *We* did the right thing. We're a crew. We're in this together." Lance put his hands on the headrest of his chair and looked down at the console. "The missile can't launch. China is safe from attack. We can deal with Global Strike Command later. We need to figure out a way to contact command post. Once they know the facts, they'll understand why we didn't launch."

"Don't bet on it," Cyndi said. "Remember the motto: No Errors, No Mistakes, No Exceptions. We'll be lucky to be thrown out of the Air Force with just a dishonorable discharge and not a court-martial." She shook her head. "Thank goodness my dad isn't alive to see this."

"We probably just prevented World War III. You don't think he'd understand why you disobeyed orders?"

"You don't get it. With my dad, good enough, never was. When I washed out of pilot training, I know I let him down. He never said that, but I could see it on his face."

"Trust me, I do understand. When I told my dad I didn't want to be a doctor, he got so bent out of shape I thought *he'd* need a heart surgeon. He didn't speak to me for weeks."

Cyndi slumped down in her chair. "Now what do I do? I wrote the book for the new combined site. I got perfect scores on every test. I was Instructor of the Year, for Christ's sake. Lot of good that did me." She buried her head in her hands.

Lance came over and put his hand on her shoulder. "Don't be so hard on yourself. It can't be easy being the commander. Especially for a woman. Act feminine, and they say you're not tough enough. Act like a guy, and they still don't let you into the bro club."

She looked up and removed his hand. "Thanks for the pep talk, but my gender has nothing to do with it. I don't play the gender card. Ever."

"Hey, just trying to help." Lance took his seat and stowed his thick binder back on the shelf. "Well, what do we do now? There's no checklist for almost nuking China."

"I'll try the commercial line." Cyndi went over to the phone on the wall and dialed the base operator. When she picked up, Cyndi said, "This is site Alpha One, I need to talk to command post."

Suddenly, the speaker on the console came alive. The creepy female voice announced, "Launch time parameters exceeded. Override protocol activated."

# CHAPTER 25

Cyndi slammed the phone down. "What happened? Did you touch something?"

Lance held up his hands like a Vegas poker dealer proving he hadn't pocketed a chip. "I didn't touch a thing." He studied the console. "The computer seems to be…"

One by one, the launch progress lights on the panel lit up.

"Launch checklist initiated," the voice said.

Under specific circumstances the system was designed to automatically launch missiles if it determined that the entire command structure had been wiped out by an attack. The thinking was that at least some of the missiles would be able to retaliate in a worst-case scenario.

"What the hell is going on?" Lance said in a panic. "The computer is trying to launch our missile."

"This can't be happening. I put the missile back in safe mode to stop this very contingency. The system can't override it." Cyndi looked at the safe mode button. The light was out. She stabbed at it repeatedly. The light wouldn't come back on.

The computer voice rattled off each step to launch a thermonuclear missile as cavalierly as it would have announced each floor in a department store elevator.

"Pull the launch key out!"

Cyndi grabbed the key and pulled. "It won't come out!" She wiggled the key then pulled with all her might. The head of the key snapped off. Its shaft remained inserted in the slot.

Cyndi frantically flipped through the pages in her binder looking for a procedure to avert Armageddon.

"Commencing countdown."

"Enter the stand down command!" she yelled.

"Ten."

Lance quickly typed in the command.

"Nine."

"It's not accepting it!"

"Eight."

"Then retarget the missile for Kwajalein Atoll," Cyndi commanded.

"Seven."

Lance typed like his life depended on it.

"Six."

"The data cable has already detached from the side of the missile! I can't change the target!"

"Five."

"We can't let it launch!" Cyndi screamed.

"Four."

"Screw this. Stand back!" Lance jumped up and snatched his gun off the worktable.

"Three."

BAM! BAM! BAM!

He gripped his Beretta with both hands and fired wildly into the REACT console.

Cyndi dove out of her chair to avoid being hit by shrapnel.

"Two."

Sparks flew. Monitor screens exploded. Smoke gushed out of the console.

"One."

Lance fired every bullet left in the clip then threw his gun at the console in a final act of desperation.

"Zero."

# CHAPTER 26

"ZERO."

"Zero."

"Zero."

The disembodied voice kept repeating the number.

Cyndi and Lance stood frozen in place. They listened for the thundering roar of the missile leaving its silo.

But the only sound they heard was the popping and crackling sound of fried circuit boards shorting out.

"Zero."

"Zero."

And that damn nagging voice of the computer repeating the name of the placeholder numeral that represents nothing.

"Shut the hell up!" Cyndi drew her pistol and blasted the speaker.

The creepy female voice fell silent.

"Thank you. Now what?" Lance asked.

Miles of ancient wiring—coated in plastic—had been shorting out and overheating after Lance blasted the rogue console. Unseen fires, fueled by melting plastic, had erupted behind the panel. Smoke, toxic fumes from combustion, and the repulsive smell of burned plastic poured out of the console.

Lance blinked, trying to wash away the stinging sensation in his eyes. His lungs burned with each breath. He began to cough uncontrollably.

It didn't take long for Cyndi and Lance to realize they were trapped in a concrete tomb sixty feet underground that was rapidly filling with poisonous air.

"Smoke hoods!" Cyndi commanded.

They rushed to pouches attached to the wall and pulled out their only chance at survival. Cyndi and Lance knelt on the floor to get under the cloud of lethal smoke while they unpacked their hoods.

They spread the elastic neck seals apart and slipped the hoods down over their heads. Activated charcoal filters did their job and cleansed each gasp for air.

Cyndi crawled on all fours to a nearby fire extinguisher and yanked it off its wall mount. She aimed the hose, squeezed the trigger, and blanketed the console with white extinguishing agent. Then she put the tip of the nozzle inside a hole in the panel and hosed down the internal fires until the extinguisher was empty.

The fires died out, but toxic smoke had filled the LCC.

"Open the blast door!" she yelled from behind the copper-colored face pane on the hood.

Lance pressed the door button on the console. Their only pathway to safety, a four-foot-thick reinforced blast door, remained tightly sealed shut. "Crap, the door circuit must be fried!" He felt his way across the smoke-filled room until he found a small metal door on the wall. Lance opened it and pumped the handle inside the box. At an excruciatingly slow rate, hydraulic pressure built up in the alternate door opening mechanism. It took thirty minutes of nonstop pumping to get enough pressure to open the eight-ton door halfway.

Poisonous smoke drifted out from the LCC and spread across the ceiling in the hallway. The air below had an acrid smell but was mostly safe to breathe.

Cyndi and Lance removed their hoods but kept them within arm's reach.

"We have to find a way to contact the base. Try the

high-frequency radio," Cyndi suggested.

Lance lifted a microphone from its cradle. The end of the coiled cord swung freely. He'd shot right through the cord while preventing the computer from starting World War III.

"This isn't going to do us any good." He tossed the microphone onto the desk. Lance gestured dramatically at all the carnage. "Well, this sucks." He looked at Cyndi with a mischievous smirk. "You think they're going to dock my pay for the damage?"

Unimaginable amounts of stress, adrenaline, and fear had suddenly found a convenient reason to leave her body. At hearing Lance's lame joke Cyndi burst into hysterical laughter. She laughed harder than she had ever laughed before. A few moments later, with the immediate danger over, she decided to chime in with her own attempt at humor. "I've got bad news for you, steely eyed missile man, you're going to be making payments on this mess for the next two million years."

Lance didn't care how corny her joke was. He cracked up laughing.

They traded more jokes and laughed like giddy children until the artificial euphoria had faded away. Then reality set in.

Cyndi plopped down in her seat, let out a deep breath, and shook her head. "We are so screwed."

"We didn't screw up anything. I'm positive something went wrong with this new system." Ever the optimist, Lance said, "We followed our hearts. That's got to count for something."

"I'll be sure to mention that at our court-martial. Maybe the Air Force will just forget the whole thing, pat us on the head, and wish us well in our civilian lives."

The view from a topside camera aimed at the front gate and helipad was displayed on a monitor on the wall. Snow covering the ground suddenly came alive. It gently swirled around in the Wyoming wind. Then the snow erupted like it had been caught up in a tornado.

The shape of a helicopter appeared in the center of the snow tornado. It hovered one foot above the helipad for a moment then touched down on the right side.

Without any sound accompanying it, the scene on the monitor had a dreamlike feel to it. The classic whap-whap-whap sound from the helicopter blades—or any other sound, for that matter—could never penetrate that far underground. A nuclear bomb could explode topside, and the only indication in the LCC would be momentary flash of light on the screen.

Lance gestured toward the monitor. "The maintenance crew is here." He glanced back at the smoldering console. "Looks like they're going to be here for a while."

"That's great," Cyndi replied with sarcasm dripping from her voice. "Goodbye, freedom."

The rotors on the helicopter slowly spun down and stopped.

Rather than settle gently back down to earth, the snowflakes erupted again in another cloud of white. A second shape appeared.

Lance tilted his head and pointed at the monitor. "Why are there two helicopters?"

# CHAPTER 27

L ANCE WALKED CLOSER and tapped the screen. "That's weird. Those aren't Grey Wolf helicopters."

After the snow had settled, two AH-6M Special Operations helicopters were visible on the screen.

Both were heavily armed.

The lead helicopter was missing a Stinger missile from its left pylon.

Major Pierce stepped out of the first helicopter and slipped on a pair of stylish Oakley sunglasses. Just because he was a trained killer, that didn't mean looking cool wasn't important. The sunglasses also provided a more practical operational benefit: They prevented the enemy from seeing his eyes and gleaning any hints of his intentions. Pierce scanned the desolate landscape. Not a single building or home was in sight. He nodded and almost smiled. "Perfect."

His copilot and the two men from the other helicopter gathered around Pierce. They were obviously geared up for a pitched battle. No name tags, unit patches, rank insignia, or anything that could help identify them was attached to their uniforms.

Members of the secretive Delta Force were culled from the top performers in the other Special Operations units. They were some of the most dangerous predators on earth.

O'Brian was a fair-skinned redhead from Boston with no neck and wide shoulders.

Jackson had survived the tough streets of the South Side of Chicago and had the physique of a bodybuilder.

Lopez was straight out of Compton. He was thin and wiry—like a cobra.

"No survivors," Pierce calmly instructed his men. "This one is personal."

"Roger that," they all replied in unison.

"After the mission, we split up and meet back at the safe house in Guadalajara."

His men held out their fists.

Pierce added his.

They bumped fists. "For Johnson! Hooah!"

———◆———

"You better take a look at this." Lance waved Cyndi over to the monitor.

She looked up at the screen. "Must be a security team from the base to guard the exposed warhead. The maintenance crew should be arriving soon."

"Global Strike Command sure doesn't screw around. These guys look like they mean business," Lance observed.

———◆———

The team spread out and took up defensive positions around the gate.

Pierce opened the intercom box and lifted the handset. He glared into the camera with a fierce expression. "Command post is aware of the problem. We're here to secure the site and escort you back to the base. Open the gate."

———◆———

"Thank God. Let's get the hell out of here." Lance reached for the button to open the gate.

"Wait." Cyndi grabbed his wrist. "I want out of here as

badly as you do, but nobody gets through the gate without valid orders. You know that."

"Screw procedure. These guys are our ride out of this hell hole," Lance shot back.

She ignored him and pressed a button on the monitor. "State everyone's full names and the entry authorization code."

---

The special operations team snickered at being asked to provide their real names.

Their leader decided it wouldn't matter. Dead men can't tell tales, as the saying goes. "This is Major Pierce. My team and I are on direct orders from General McNeil back at headquarters. Now open the damned gate."

Cyndi's reply boomed from the intercom. "I'm not allowed to open the gate without a valid entry code! I'm only going to ask you one more time. State your names and entry code."

Pierce didn't respond. He hung up and closed the door on the intercom box.

---

"We need to call headquarters and find out if these guys are legit." Cyndi hurried over to the phone on the wall. She dialed the base operator. When she picked up, Cyndi said in a panicked voice, "This is site Alpha One. I need to talk to—"

Static intruded on the call.

"What? I can't hear you," the operator said.

"This is an emergency! I need to talk to General McNeil at headquarters right away!" Cyndi yelled.

"Hold please."

"Wait! You don't understand—" Cyndi's response wasn't fast enough to keep the secretary on the line. Serene Muzak played, informing Cyndi that in her time of dire need she'd been put on hold.

———◆———

Lola Crawford buzzed in on the intercom. "General, someone is calling for you on line two. They say it's an emergency."

"Who is it?" he replied.

"I'm not a mind reader, General. All I know is they said it was an emergency," came her snotty reply.

General McNeil cussed her under his breath then picked up his phone. "Who is this?"

"General, this is Capt. Cyndi Stafford. I'm the commander out at site Alpha One. There's been a serious emergency."

"What the hell are you talking about? What kind of emergency?"

Cyndi hesitated, thinking of a tactful way to phrase the worst news she could possibly deliver to the commander of 90th Missile Wing. "Well, sir, we received an Emergency Action Message…but the thing is…we couldn't tell if it was—"

Static hissed in her ear.

"Speak up, Captain. I can't understand you," McNeil said.

"The REACT console malfunctioned, and…" Cyndi decided it was futile trying to explain everything that had happened over a terrible connection. "I can explain later." She focused on the most pressing issue. "There's a Major Pierce at the gate. He says he's here on direct orders from you to bring us back to the base. But he doesn't have a gate entry code. What do you want me to do?"

"Who's trying to get access to the site?"

"Pierce, sir. Major Pierce."

McNeil lowered the phone and covered the mouthpiece. "Shit." Perspiration suddenly coated his forehead. He wiped it away with the back of his hand. McNeil put the phone back up to his ear. "Captain, you did the smart thing in calling me. I knew I picked the right missileer for the job. I never gave any order for Pierce to go to Alpha One. That lunatic must have gone rogue. He's out to avenge the death of his friend, Sergeant Johnson. Under no circumstances are you to allow Pierce to enter the grounds. I order you to use deadly force to defend the—"

The line went silent.

"Hello? General, are you there?" Cyndi tapped the switch hook on the phone, trying to reestablish the connection. "General McNeil, are you there?"

Cyndi glared at the receiver as if it would suddenly start working again just to mollify her.

She slammed the phone back into its cradle. "Dammit! The line's dead."

"What did he say!" Lance asked in a panic.

"McNeil never ordered Pierce to come out here. He must have gone rogue." Cyndi picked up Lance's Beretta and handed it to him. "Put in a fresh clip."

# CHAPTER 28

CYNDI AND LANCE went back to the monitor. Pierce and his men were nowhere to be seen.

"Switch cameras," Cyndi instructed her deputy.

He rotated the camera selection knob on the monitor. The grounds near the code burner were empty. The area around the two-thousand-gallon diesel fuel tank showed no signs of life. He switched to the view of the silo blast door.

"Jesus! They're coming through the fence," Lance shouted.

The four Delta Force operators were belly crawling through the snow and under the breach in the fence created by the door. As they stood up, each man went off in different directions. The scene on the monitor was empty again.

Then the picture went dead.

Lance rotated the knob, looking for a working camera. "They've cut the lines. We're completely blind."

They listened for any sounds that would give away the team's location.

It didn't take long.

The sound of C-4 explosives obliterating the door to the building above reverberated down the elevator shaft. Dust and debris rained down into the hallway.

"Close the blast door!" Cyndi yelled.

Lance flipped the selector switch in the box to Close, grabbed the handle with both hands, and pumped frantically.

A snail crawling across the floor would have moved faster than the blast door.

They heard a metallic banging echo through the hallway. The steel lattice elevator door had just been slammed closed. The electric motor powering the elevator came to life. Pierce and his team were coming for them.

Realizing the futility of trying to close the massive door in time, Cyndi said, "Split up. Take cover on your side. Wait for my order before firing."

Lance went down on one knee to the left of the blast doorframe.

Cyndi got in position on the right side.

The smoke-filled hallway obscured her view of the elevator shaft. Unable to see more than a few feet, she tilted an ear toward the hallway.

Seconds ticked off as Cyndi and Lance waited for any sign of what they were up against. All too soon, they got their answer. Loud coughing could be heard at the far end of the hallway. The Special Forces team had arrived.

Specialists in close-quarters battle, the team came armed with Heckler & Koch HK416 rifles and Glock 17 pistols—perfect for close-quarters combat. The HK416 had earned mythical status among operators after it was confirmed to be the gun used to kill Osama bin Laden.

They kicked in doors in the smokey hallway and took cover behind them. The men lay on the cold concrete floor to escape the poisonous air above. Four rifles were trained on the opening to the LCC.

"Drop your weapons!" Cyndi yelled out. Given how outgunned they were, she had delivered the order with surprising bravado.

"Hold your fire," Pierce coolly replied. "Everyone just calm down. We're here to secure the site and escort you back to base. That's all. I don't want anyone to get hurt."

Cyndi squinted into the haze, trying to make out their

locations. "Is that Major Pierce?'

"Yes, it is. Are you injured, Captain Stafford?"

"I'm fine."

"Is Lieutenant Garcia okay? I have a first aid kit if you need it."

"He's fine."

"I need Garcia to answer for himself to prove he's still alive."

Lance turned to Cyndi with a puzzled look. "Still alive? Why wouldn't I be?"

# CHAPTER 29

"GARCIA, ARE YOU okay? I need to hear your voice," Pierce repeated.

Lance pulled back from the doorway. "What the hell is he talking about?"

"I said he's fine," Cyndi shouted. She pulled back as well. "He's trying to get us to turn on each other."

"Lieutenant, if you can hear me, think about your future. She's the one responsible for what happened. Cyndi is the crew commander, not you. The buck stops with her. Give yourself up peacefully, and your pilot training slot will be held for you. Make the wrong call, and it's gone."

"How does he know about my new assignment?" Lance asked with genuine concern. "I just got the letter. And how does he know your first name?"

"How should I know?" Cyndi lay on her stomach and peeked around the door. When she saw their rifles, her eyes narrowed.

Pierce motioned to Lopez. "Talk to him."

Lopez nodded. "Garcia, you in there?" he yelled out. "*Hablas español, amigo?*"

Lance's father had come from a very wealthy family in Mexico City. Despite his privileged upbringing and the best private tutors to teach him English, he'd required his own kids to learn Spanish to maintain a connection to their heritage.

"Sí," Lance replied.

"*La chica está loca, muchacho!*"

"What did he say?" Cyndi asked.

"Don't worry about it," Lance answered. "He's pretending we're friends because I speak Spanish."

"Chica means girl, doesn't it?"

Lance rolled his eyes. "Fine. He said you're crazy. Now, are you happy?"

"Crazy? I'll show him crazy." Cyndi jumped up behind the cover of the door and drew her pistol.

Lance put a hand up. "I've got this. Let me handle it." He drew closer to the edge of the doorframe and yelled, "We're not amigos, so drop the act. Go back to the barrio where you belong, *cholo*."

"Kiss my ass, *pendejo*!" Lopez jerked his rifle up into firing position.

Pierce slapped him across the back of the helmet. "Stand down, dammit."

Inside the LCC, Cyndi chuckled. "I don't speak Spanish, but he's probably not going to buy you a beer when this is over." She flashed a thumbs-up from across the opening. "Good job getting inside his head."

"Stafford, this is Major Pierce. I read your mandatory psych eval that was done before you entered missileer training. In his report the shrink said you were a rule follower, fiercely loyal, a high achiever, and a patriot. I believe him. Let's go back to the base and sort everything out like good airmen. Do the right thing. Don't tarnish your family name any more than it already has been."

Somehow, Pierce managed to claw at Cyndi's confidence. The logical part of her brain couldn't find the strength to brush it off, despite McNeil having told her Pierce had gone rogue. Because of that nature as a rule follower, a sliver of doubt had worked its way into Cyndi's thought process, a kernel of guilt—exactly as Pierce had hoped. She sank back and slid down the blast door. Cyndi holstered her gun.

"Don't listen to his crap," Lance warned.

"What would your dad tell you to do if he were still alive?" Pierce asked with faux concern.

"Cyndi, he's messing with you."

Cyndi pulled her knees up against her chest. She looked around the LCC and shook her head in disgust. "Look what I've done."

In only a few hours she'd managed to expose a thermonuclear missile to the outside world and destroy millions of dollars' worth of Air Force hardware, not to mention both of their careers.

Some role model she was.

She could see her father's face. Disappointment was written all over it. The stern voice he'd used when he taught her to fly repeatedly played in her head. *Your plane is out of control. You're diving at the ground. What are you going to do, just give up?*

# CHAPTER 30

C YNDI STOOD UP with a fresh look of resolve on
her face. She edged closer to the door. "I don't recognize your name, Major Pierce. Are you the commander
of the 91st or 92nd Security Forces Squadron?"

"Stop stalling, Captain."

"It's important to know who I'm dealing with before I
make any decisions. Which squadron, Major?"

"What difference does it make which one I command?
The reason you don't recognize my name is because I
just transferred to Warren."

Lance looked over at Cyndi and smiled.

She winked at him. "Well, Major, the reason it matters
is because there is no 91st or 92nd squadron at Warren."

"Shit," Pierce mumbled under his breath.

"I'm guessing from your guns you guys are SEALs?
Maybe Delta Force?"

"Enough!" Pierce jumped up. "There's no way out
of here except past us. You're trapped and you know it.
Come out with your hands up, and you won't be harmed.
That's an order, Captain."

"You're not in my chain of command. You might outrank me, but down here I'm in charge. I say what goes.
Not you."

"General McNeil sure as hell outranks you. He gave
me direct orders to bring you two back to the base, and
that's what I'm going to do."

"Strike two, genius!" Cyndi yelled mockingly. "I just

talked to the general on the phone. He said you've gone rogue. He said he didn't authorize any of this."

Pierce went silent as he reassessed his adversaries.

"That prick sold us out," Jackson growled to his leader.

"McNeil is probably sending a security team to the site right now," O'Brian stated nervously. "These two get out of here, and we're headed to prison."

"Shut the hell up," Pierce barked. "The missile is still in the silo. We're gonna finish what we came here to do. Follow my lead."

"What about McNeil?" Lopez questioned.

"Like I said, no survivors." A chilling smirk spread across his face. "He's mine." Pierce slipped his Glock 17 into his waistband behind his back. "Hold your fire! I'm coming out!" he yelled down the hallway.

A shape appeared in the smokey hallway.

Cyndi gulped when she saw the size of the man. His hulking frame was silhouetted against the smoke by the ceiling lights behind him. His face remained hidden in darkness. "Drop your weapon!" she yelled.

"Yes, ma'am. It's your show down here." Pierce put his rifle down and kicked it away. "I'm unarmed. Don't do anything stupid."

"Tell your men to toss their rifles into the hallway," Cyndi ordered.

"Like hell I will," O'Brian said.

Pierce looked back. "Do it!"

His men reluctantly slid their HK416s into the hallway.

Pierce moved forward in a casual, friendly gait toward the LCC. He flashed the wide smile of a used-car salesman. "Look, I don't know what General McNeil said, but obviously there's been a huge misunderstanding. Let me in. We'll get him back on the phone and get all of this straightened out."

"Stop where you are!" Lance yelled.

Pierce stopped.

Lance leaned back away from the opening. "He's not getting in here."

"Lance! We're outnumbered and outgunned," Cyndi shot back.

She had no illusions they could successfully take on four Delta Force operatives with only their Berettas and no close-quarters combat training.

"What other choice do we have? Even if McNeil is right about Pierce going rogue, we can still use him as a bargaining chip to get out of here alive." She turned and spoke to the shadowy figure in the hall. "Keep your hands where I can see them. You're going to come into the LCC alone, then we're closing the blast door."

"Smart decision, Captain. In a minute, this will be all over." Pierce started forward.

"Turn around," Cyndi said. "Put your hands on your head and walk backward into the LCC."

"Crap," Jackson murmured as he looked around at his teammates.

Pierce raised his hands. His jaw tightened. "Relax, Stafford. You can see I'm unarmed."

"Do what I said! Turn around!"

"Get ready," Lopez whispered to the others.

"How do I know you won't just shoot me in the back?"

"If you don't turn around, I'll shoot you in the front," Lance declared, hoping to intimidate the trained killer.

Pierce slowly lowered his hands toward his back. "I'm going to get a radio so my team can stay in contact with me after you close the door. They need to know that I'm safe." Pierce flashed a hand signal to his team as he turned.

Lopez stood and removed a radio from his vest. He held it out for Pierce.

"No! Slide it to me!" Cyndi shouted.

Lopez looked at Pierce.

He nodded.

Lopez slid the radio down the hall and up to the blast door.

Cyndi leaned out to pick up the radio.

With impossible speed, Pierce reached behind his back.

"Gun!" Lance screamed.

# CHAPTER 31

IN A BLUR, Pierce snatched his pistol from his waistband. As he drew a bead on Cyndi, Lance catapulted across the opening and pushed her back behind the door.

A shot rang out.

The slug from the Glock hit Lance instead.

He collapsed on the floor.

Cyndi drew her Beretta, stuck it out around the door, and unleashed a volley of cover fire. With no idea where she was aiming, bullets ricocheted off the concrete floor and walls. Ceiling lights in the path of the bullets exploded in a white-hot shower of sparks.

"Cover me!" Pierce dove for cover.

His men crawled into the hallway and grabbed their rifles, ignoring the deadly projectiles. As soon as they got back behind cover, they switched their HK416s to full auto.

All hell broke loose.

Ten rounds a second gushed from each of the three weapons. The deafening sound of gunfire reverberated off the solid walls in the confined space. Pierce crawled back to safety and added to the fusillade of firepower.

Bullets pinged off the massive blast door like annoying gnats. The ones that made it through the opening shattered after hitting the steel-reinforced capsule walls. Lead fragments and bits of concrete whizzed by the missileers, creating even more lethal threats to their survival.

Cyndi dragged Lance away from the opening, leaving

behind a trail of blood. She lay across his prone body to protect him. "Lance, can you hear me? Are you okay?" she whispered.

"Been better," he answered through clenched teeth. Lance was clutching his right thigh. When he pulled his hands away, thick crimson liquid coated them. Two holes in the leg of his flight suit were leaking blood. The bullet had passed through his upper thigh, missing the femoral artery by mere inches.

Cyndi propped him up against the wall. She grabbed the first aid kit and wrapped the wound with gauze. When he was lucid enough to become aware of his surroundings, Cyndi sat next to him and cradled him in her arms. "Why did you do that? You're so stupid. You could've been killed."

"Isn't it obvious?" he weakly replied.

"No."

Lance forced a grin. "If you got shot, who'd teach yoga class?"

Cyndi looked lovingly into his deep brown eyes and shook her head. "You have the worst comedic timing of anyone I've ever met." Despite her annoyance with his ill-timed sense of humor, she leaned down and planted a kiss on his lips. When their lips parted, she asked, "Can you shoot?"

"I think so." He pulled himself over to the edge of the blast door and squeezed off a few rounds.

All this accomplished was to draw a fresh barrage of lead from the Delta team again.

Cyndi and Lance returned fire as best they could, given the overwhelming firepower they faced. The few remaining ceiling lights were shot out. They ejected their empty clips, jammed in their last ones, and continued firing.

The entire underground fortress was filled with gun smoke. The dark, hazy conditions made it impossible to see their targets down the hallway. Cyndi slowly angled her head closer to the blast door, squinting, straining to see through all the smoke. *Great*, she thought, *this place was going to be my crypt.*

Cyndi fired off a few more errant shots then pulled back behind the door. "This isn't working."

"We're just wasting ammo," Lance responded.

"Hold your fire, I'm going to find a way out of here."

Not hearing any shots, the team members slowly crept out from behind their cover. Four large figures entered the smokey hallway. They crouched down and advanced toward the LCC.

Lance saw movement in the hallway. He turned to Cyndi and excitedly announced, "Here they come!"

O'Brian and Jackson lead the team down the hallway.

"Hurry!" Lance yelled.

Out of ideas, and nearly out of ammo, Cyndi searched the LCC. In an act of desperation, she grabbed a fire extinguisher off its wall bracket and hurtled it down the hall.

Unable to discern what the metal object was that was bouncing toward them, O'Brian panicked and yelled, "Grenade!"

The four men dove for the floor and scrambled back to safety.

"What the hell is that supposed to do?" Lance asked with a puzzled look.

"Trust me," Cyndi replied.

Seconds ticked by as they peered out into the smoky hallway.

An overdose of adrenaline coursed through the veins of the hyper-aggressive alpha males. They were programmed for action, and now they were reduced to cowering behind doorframes, waiting for the next move from a couple of wimpy missileers.

Ultimately, their colossal egos got the best of them.

O'Brian jumped up. "I've had enough of this. We're coming for you, assholes!"

He and Jackson sprinted toward the LCC.

# CHAPTER 32

"**N**OW!" CYNDI SCREAMED.
The two took aim at the fire extinguisher and let loose a volley of lead.

Just before exhausting their final clips, the pressurized vessel exploded, spewing out white powder and a shower of jagged shrapnel.

Pierce instinctively turned away from the blast, using his helmet to shield his face. When he attempted to get up, he felt a searing pain in his leg. A hot chunk of metal had imbedded itself in his calf. Without so much as a wince of pain, he yanked it out and tossed it aside. The team leader crawled across the floor until reaching the safety of the small room. Once inside, he tilted his head out of the doorway and whispered, "Team, report your status."

"Good to go," Lopez replied from the room across the hall.

Ominous silence filled the damp air. Burned sulfur from the gunpowder had filled the space with a repulsive smell similar to rotten eggs.

Pierce squinted, trying to see through the dim haze.

"O'Brian. Jackson. Report your status!" he repeated in a stern but hushed voice.

No response.

The phrase *fog of war* was never more valid than here in this subterranean battlefield. The dim hallway was filled with gun smoke, white extinguisher agent, dust, and fumes from the console fire. Intelligent tactical decisions became nearly impossible.

"That bitch!" Pierce blurted out. Absent a response from his men, Pierce didn't waste any time mourning their fate. He assumed they were dead and proceeded with his original plan. He flashed hand signals at Lopez.

The few bulbs that remained lit in the LCC provided a glaring backdrop in contrast to the dark hallway. Pierce and Lopez unleashed another barrage of bullets on the opening.

Cyndi and Lance stayed safely tucked behind the partially closed blast door as the bullets flew. Fragments from the rounds struck the phone hanging on the wall, shattering it.

She reached up and flipped off the light switch, plunging the entire underground complex into total darkness.

The operators reacted by simply lowering their helmet-mounted night-vision goggles over their eyes. The pitch-black scene took on an eerie green glow. They continued firing into the LCC, creating a blinding strobe light effect with their muzzle flashes.

Cyndi took a small penlight flashlight out of her flight suit pocket and shined it at Lance. He was slumped back against the wall. The temporary field dressing on his leg had bled completely through. She grabbed him by the shoulder, "Stay with me. I need you. I can't hold off these guys alone."

He mumbled something unintelligible.

With bullets flying all around them, Cyndi kept her head down and quickly removed the blood-soaked gauze from his leg and tossed it aside. Lance writhed in pain as she wrapped his leg with a fresh dressing.

After she'd finished, Cyndi looked at him and shook her head. "You're no good to me this way." She grabbed a syringe labeled *MORPHINE* from the first aid kit and removed the protective cap over the needle. "Time to cowboy up, Tex." She didn't bother being gentle. Cyndi jabbed the needle through his flight suit and into his thigh, just above the wound. She injected an amount that she thought would deaden the pain but not render Lance useless in their battle against Pierce and his men.

Lance flinched and let out an anguished moan. He wasn't sure if his clouded mind had processed the situation correctly, but he thought he saw a smile on Cyndi's face as she administered the painful shot.

The powerful narcotic took effect almost immediately. Pain from the gunshot wound slowly receded. Lance was able to stand with Cyndi's help.

With his arm draped across her shoulder, she helped Lance over to a chair at the console. He sat down and gingerly poked at the wound. "What do we do now?"

Her deputy was injured, they were almost out of ammo, and they were fumbling around in the dark.

And their opponents were highly skilled assassins with night-vision goggles.

Suddenly, putting up with her overbearing mother back in LA didn't seem like such a bad alternative.

Cyndi was overcome with feelings of dejection. She let out a heavy sigh. "If we want to come out of this alive, I only see one option."

"We're in this together," Lance said. "You lead; I'll follow."

Cyndi crept over to the door. From behind safe cover she yelled, "Major Pierce, this is Captain Stafford! Are you out there? Are you still alive?"

Hearing her voice, Pierce raised his rifle. He moved it in tandem with his NVGs as he scanned the opening, looking for movement. "Sorry to disappoint you, sweet cheeks, but I'm still very much alive. And so are all my men. Your little stunt with the extinguisher backfired."

"Hey, you can't blame me for trying," she responded flippantly. "We've held off the best of the best, but I know when I'm beat. I've decided to surrender. But only on my terms."

"I don't think you're in any position to be dictating how this is going to end, Stafford."

"Have it your way. I'll just close the blast door and wait you clowns out. We have two months of food and water in here." Exploiting their lack of knowledge about the condition of the LCC, she turned toward Lance and yelled, "Close the door!"

"Wait!" Never having been in a launch control center before, Pierce saw his opportunity to complete his mission slipping away.

"Smart decision, Major." Cyndi summoned up all her confidence as she continued. "These are my conditions. When we leave here, you are to take us directly to General McNeil. I want a security team in place to guard the missile before we leave. My deputy, Lieutenant Garcia, is injured. He will need to be carried out. No one is to enter the LCC until I've had a chance to tend to his wounds."

"Your concern for the well-being of your deputy is touching," Pierce said in a snide tone. "I accept your terms."

"I'm not finished," Cyndi shot back. "I want your assurance no harm will come to me or Lance once we surrender."

His cold, dead eyes smiled. "You have my word. You will not be harmed."

# CHAPTER 33

"THANK YOU, MAJOR. I need to change the bandage on his leg. Give me five minutes," Cyndi shouted.

"You have two. Throw your guns into the hallway first," Pierce ordered. "I don't want any nasty surprises when we come in."

There was no response from the LCC.

Pierce was about to repeat his order when a Beretta pistol slid across the floor. Moments later a second gun came sliding toward him.

Out of an abundance of caution he left them where they came to rest. Pierce slapped a new thirty round mag into his rifle. He signaled Lopez to do the same.

While waiting for his prey to voluntarily walk into his trap, Pierce leaned back against the wall. He removed his Ops-Core ballistic helmet and turned his head to the side, taking a draw on the tube leading to his hydration backpack.

Thoughts of a carefree life on the beach, with one or two Mexican beauties satisfying his every need, briefly flashed across his mind. Unlike the average man, the tantalizing thoughts left as quickly as they had come. Pierce was no average man. Being out of the game wasn't an option for him.

He'd been orphaned at four years old when his parents had died in a fiery car crash at 2 a.m. coming home from a bar. After no relatives stepped forward to claim him, a neighbor took him to the police station and dumped him on the front steps with a note pinned to his shirt. Pierce grew up bouncing from family to family in the brutal world of the foster care system. Every relationship he'd ever had eventually crashed and burned. The realization that not one single person on the outside cared if he was dead or alive had hardened his heart even more.

The *life*, despite its obvious drawbacks, was all he had. And even that was tenuous. He knew his handlers wouldn't lose a minute of sleep over sacrificing him if it achieved their goals for the next foreign policy crisis du jour.

Today would be different. The days of being treated like a disposable pawn were over. It was his turn to play God.

After he'd accomplished his mission, remaining with Delta Force was not possible, of course. Fortunately, there was no shortage of corrupt politicians, corporate executives that feared being kidnapped, and scumbag drug lords in Mexico who would pay top dollar for a bodyguard with his skills.

They would consider him just another knuckle-dragging goon, but the money would help him overlook their condescending, misinformed judgment. His new life would allow him to stay in the game and finally live the lavish lifestyle he was entitled to after all he'd sacrificed. Still, knowing how many people were going to die today gnawed at his conscience—what little he had left of it.

Compartmentalizing the emotional fallout from what he was about to do was Pierce's way of living with his homicidal plan.

The major shook off thoughts about the course of his immediate future and snapped back to the task at hand. Growing impatient with the delay, he called out, "Times up, Stafford! Come out with your hands on your head!"

He listened for her reply.

No response came.

"Now, Stafford!"

Silence greeted his vehement demand.

Pierce strapped on his helmet and lowered the NVGs. He fired two rounds from his Glock 17 into the opening to get her attention. "Last chance, Captain. Come out or die."

Still no response.

Pierce signaled Lopez to ready a grenade.

He pulled back a strip of Velcro on his vest covering a fragmentation grenade.

Pierce shook his head. "Use a flash-bang. I don't want to destroy the launch console."

Lopez switched to the less lethal weapon.

Pierce pointed at the opening and nodded.

His teammate pulled the safety pin, crept out into the hallway, and rolled the grenade down the middle of the floor like a bowling ball.

Because of its irregular shape, the M84 stun grenade skipped and bounced down the hallway in a haphazard path. When it disappeared through the opening, Lopez dove for cover and covered the lenses of his NVGs.

The grenade went off with a deafening 180 decibels of sound and eight million candelas of blinding light. The cacophonous explosion was amplified even more when it echoed off the solid walls and ceiling.

Smoke billowed out of the opening.

Pierce and Lopez crouched low and hugged the walls as they moved forward. Halfway to the LCC they reached the corpses of their fallen comrades. A pool of dark crimson liquid was slowly spreading across the hallway. Still pointing their rifles at the LCC, they rolled the bodies over. Shrapnel from the extinguisher tank had shredded every area of exposed skin. Razor-sharp pieces had severed arteries and pierced vital organs. The men's faces were so mangled, if it weren't for the obvious difference in skin color, identifying them would have been nearly impossible.

After all the times they'd cheated death in the worst Third World hellholes there are, O'Brian and Jackson had quietly bled out and died in a dark, dank dungeon controlled by their own country.

Pierce took spare magazines off the men and left their bodies where they lay.

The surviving members of the team stood and tucked themselves against the outside of the blast door. Pierce did a quick glance into the LCC and scanned the room with his NVGs. Not seeing any movement, he waved Lopez forward.

Guns raised, they hurried into the LCC. The men spread apart as much as feasible in the small space. To avoid tunnel vision and vertigo, the operators rotated their heads slowly while they scanned the room with their NVGs.

Lopez searched the gaps between computer cabinets, under the desk, and next to the toilet.

Pierce ripped the curtain and its rod away from the bunk. It was empty. He turned and whispered, "You see their bodies?"

"Um…negative, sir," Lopez replied with puzzlement in his voice.

Pierce flipped on the light switch and ripped off his NVGs. He held a hand over his eyes and blinked rapidly until they had adjusted to the light. When they did, his dead eyes became filled with rage. "What the hell do you mean, negative? They didn't just vanish into thin air!"

When he turned and saw the console, Pierce went ballistic. "Where the hell are they!" He smashed everything in sight with the butt of his rifle.

Lopez decided to stay silent rather than add fuel to the fire by stating the obvious.

Pierce stared at the charred and bullet-ridden REACT console in disbelief. "Those bastards! I'll never be able to launch now!"

With his mission objective now out of reach, he repeatedly pounded on the solidly built console but did little additional damage. Pierce kicked at debris on the floor, like a spoiled child throwing a temper tantrum. A piece bounced off the storage cabinet door under the desk. It made a hollow, tinny sound.

Pierce stopped his tirade. He held up a hand and trained his ear on the cabinet door. He waved Lopez over. Pierce pointed two fingers at his eyes then pointed at the cabinet door.

Lopez crouched down and put his hand on the door latch.

Pierce backed away and took a knee.

He pressed the stock of his HK416 into his shoulder, leveled it at the door, and closed his left eye.

Laughing, he said, "In case you two haven't figured it out yet, I lied about letting you live."

Lopez yanked the door open.

Major Pierce unleashed a slashing volley of 5.56-caliber rounds into the large space.

# CHAPTER 34

SERGEANT MORGAN RUSHED up and knocked on the office door.

Colonel Wilmer didn't hear it. He was lost in an extremely thorough inventory of the training-scenario SD cards stored in his desk drawer.

Morgan knocked harder.

Wilmer looked up with a scowl on his face. "I'm busy. Go away!"

Morgan ignored the rude comment and opened the door. He held out a stack of computer printouts. "Sir, I've checked all the major systems in the command post. There were no malfunctions in any of our equipment."

With a panicked voice, Wilmer said, "Then run a systems check on Alpha One. Check comms, check missile status, check the feeds from the security cameras." He jumped up. "Check everything, dammit!"

◆

Embarrassment combined with rage kept Pierce blasting away into the empty storage cabinet until his clip was empty.

Lopez held the door open and waited until the needless waste of ammo was over. He was going to say something but thought better of it when he saw the insane look in Pierce's eyes. He wisely stayed silent, got up, and started another search of the LCC.

Lopez began at the left end of the room. He moved aside a stack of manuals then stopped and looked up at the ceiling. A puzzled expression formed on his face. During his initial sweep he hadn't noticed a round metal hatch built into the ceiling.

Above it, a sixty-foot-long steel tube connected the LCC to the surface. For obvious security reasons, the existence of an alternative route for getting out of the underground bunker after an attack had been kept classified since the 1970s.

Lopez assumed their vanishing prey had gone up the emergency escape tube. Without getting clearance from Pierce first, he opened the hatch. Wet sand, designed to absorb the shock wave from a nearby blast, poured out of the three-foot-diameter tube. Fifty-four thousand pounds of sand first crushed Lopez, then suffocated him.

The tidal wave of sand knocked Pierce off his feet. He got on his hands and knees and scrambled away from the spreading pile. Once he was a safe distance away, he rolled onto his back and collapsed on the floor. Pierce stared up at the ceiling, pounded his fists on the floor, and screamed, "Fuck!"

The sense of impotency Pierce felt lying on his back with nothing to show for it was obvious. His curses echoed off the solid LCC walls until it ricocheted back and struck Pierce squarely in the ego.

Months of planning his revenge for the death of his only friend had gone up in smoke. His team was dead, the console was too damaged to use, the missile remained in the silo, his career with Delta Force was over, a security team was likely on its way, and most infuriating of all, the two missileers had somehow turned into ghosts and vanished into thin air.

He closed his eyes and tried to focus his mind on his next steps. A faint sound caught his attention. Pierce opened his eyes and turned his head to the side. The layer of sand on the floor was slowly disappearing like sand running through an hourglass. He got up and looked at the strange pattern. The missing grains of sand formed a perfect grid across the floor.

Pierce knelt and brushed away the sand. He thumped each tile on the floor with his fist. One of the tiles bounced slightly. He pushed down on its corner, which raised up the far end. Sand poured into the opening. Pierce lifted the tile and flung it away.

Miles of new wiring needed to be installed between the old LCC and the new missile silo. A raised platform had been built to provide a pathway for it all. The new floor was eighteen inches above the original concrete floor.

Pierce pulled out his flashlight and pointed it down the wiring tunnel. In a quick move, he put his head into the opening then pulled it back in case his targets were still armed. In that brief moment he was able to see a small beam of light and two dark shapes far down the tunnel moving away from him.

———◆———

A burst of optimism had invigorated Lance when Cyndi had shown him the wiring tunnel. The morphine was doing its job blocking the pain in his leg, so he didn't hesitate to leave the LCC. He scrambled forward on his stomach as fast as possible in the confined space.

Cyndi was right behind him. She saw a beam of light flash by. "Get your ass in gear, Lancelot. Pierce just discovered the wiring tunnel."

Gunshots rang out. Bullets whizzed by their heads. Pierce was firing blindly down the tunnel.

The sound of each shot echoed in the confined space. As deafening as the noise was, it beat getting hit by a 9 mm slug. The ringing in their ears would go away. A direct hit to a vital organ would spell doom.

So far, luck was smiling on them.

———◆———

Pierce pulled his gun back out of the tunnel and jammed in a new clip. He was much bigger than either of the missileers. To have any hope of fitting in the confined crawl space he'd have to get rid of every piece of protective equipment he had. The rifle was useless. He stripped off his helmet, tactical knee and elbow pads, and vest. Only his pistol and flashlight would accompany him. He crammed himself into the space headfirst. Sheer determination, and seething anger at his prey for escaping his grasp, propelled him forward down the small tunnel.

Any concerns about claustrophobia had been stripped from his consciousness years ago by the cruel methods of confinement repeatedly administered during the six-month Operator Training Course. That part of the training had washed out more candidates than any other.

———◆———

Lance stopped when he bumped his head into something. He'd reached the end of the tunnel. He banged his knuckles on the flat surface. The unmistakable sound of metal reverberated off the steel plate. He pounded on it with his fists. The plate didn't budge.

The tunnel had widened slightly at the end to accommodate the thick cables curving left and right as they went off to their assigned equipment. The thick plate covered an opening in the silo wall that allowed maintenance crews to access the wiring.

Lance tucked himself into a ball and slowly spun himself around until his feet faced the plate. With his good leg, he kicked at it with all his might. The plate still didn't budge. "Help me," he told Cyndi.

She banged on the plate with her fists while Lance kicked. Her efforts did little to help. Cyndi tried to rotate her body around but was unable to with Lance filling most of the cramped space.

"Hug me," he said unexpectedly.

"What?" Cyndi replied with disbelief. "We have a maniac with a gun coming after us, and that's where your brain is?"

In the dark tunnel, Lance winked. "Maybe later. Right now, we need to figure out a way to fit two bodies in a space only big enough for one. I'll lie flat. You climb on top of me. We'll wriggle around until your feet are facing the plate. Then you can help me kick it."

"Oh…right," Cyndi said sheepishly.

She lay across Lance. Their bodies twisted and inter-twined in ways that would make a contortionist blush.

Finally, Cyndi's feet were facing the metal plate. A bullet ricocheted off the plate just as they were about to kick. With renewed motivation, they slammed their feet against it. A corner bent outward. A hopeful ray of light shone through. More kicks bent a second corner.

"Harder!" Lance yelled.

Two more kicks, and the plate fell away, clanging against the concrete below as it landed.

Cyndi poked her head out the opening. A layer of dense fog began right below the opening, obscuring the view of the silo floor. She had no way of gauging how far the drop was. Cyndi looked out at the sixty-foot-tall Minuteman missile. It appeared that the opening was located about halfway up the missile. Jumping down thirty feet without knowing if the floor were clear of any equipment or if there was a floor at all in this section of the silo would be suicide.

Cyndi looked up. Brilliant blue Wyoming sky filled the large opening. Snowflakes swirled around in the wind. As enticing an escape option as the opening would have been to solve their predicament, the smooth silo walls made it impossible to climb to safety. They might as well have been at the bottom of a deep concrete well.

She looked over to her left. The data cable that had been attached to the missile umbilical dangled down, four feet away from her. The remaining cable disappeared into the fog. There was no way to tell if it reached the floor.

Cyndi turned to face the silo wall. She leaned to her right and reached out as far as she could. The thick cable was only six inches from her outstretched hand.

She ducked back into the tunnel and asked, "Do you trust me?"

Lance's eyes narrowed. "Is this one of those trick questions women like to ask?"

Cyndi didn't have time for his jokes. "The data transfer cable is next to the opening. We can shimmy down it to the silo floor. You're taller than me, but with your injured leg I doubt you can do the gyrations necessary to reach it. I need your help."

Lance stuck his head out the opening. "I see what you mean."

"That's why you're going to have to trust me. With your help I should be able to reach the cable. After I reach the floor, I'll swing the cable over to you."

"What if the cable ends just below the fog? You'll break every bone in your body dropping to the floor. Neither of us has ever been in a missile silo before. Who knows what might be down there?"

Sounds of Pierce struggling to crawl through the narrow tunnel grew louder.

"I can't promise you this will work"—Cyndi pointed back down the dark tunnel—"but if we stay here, we die." She cupped his hand in hers. "I'm willing to take the leap of faith if you are."

Lance was certain there was a double entendre hidden somewhere in her last sentence, but a bullet whistling past his ear persuaded him to concentrate on their only option for survival. "Time to go!"

Cyndi maneuvered her body out of the opening and stood on the bottom edge. Lance provided the anchor by grabbing her left wrist. She grabbed his wrist as well.

Lance could feel her pounding heartbeat in her wrist. "Are you okay?"

"Don't worry; I've got this." Her trembling voice was less than reassuring.

Facing the wall, Cyndi extended her right arm. The cable was still out of reach. She leaned to her right. The pathway to surviving their deadly dilemma was now only two inches from her grasp. "A little more. I've almost got it."

Lance extended his arm as far as he could.

Cyndi lifted her right foot off the edge and swung her leg out to help extend her reach.

Just as she opened her hand to grab the cable, Cyndi's left foot slipped.

She disappeared into the dense fog.

# CHAPTER 35

ANGLING BY HER left arm, she bounced off the silo wall. "Don't let go!" she yelled.

"I've got you!"

Cyndi thrashed around trying to gain a foothold on anything projecting from the smooth silo wall.

Her weight threatened to pull Lance out of the opening and plunge both to their deaths. He braced his feet against the sides of the opening and sat up. Lance reached down and grabbed Cyndi's wrist with both hands.

She reached up and clamped on to his arm with her free hand. Her sweaty palm made it hard to get a firm grasp.

Lance looked down at the surreal scene. Cyndi was swaying in and out of the fog. The top half of a thermonuclear missile, that may or may not ignite at any moment, loomed a few feet away. And a bloodthirsty Special Forces commander was getting closer by the second.

Lance had joined the Air Force for the adventure, but this was a bit much.

"Swing me over to the cable!" Cyndi yelled. "I'm going to hook it with my foot!"

Lance swung Cyndi back and forth like the pendulum in a grandfather clock. She looked over at the cable visible above the fog to help gauge her distance from it. On the third swing she decided she was getting close. Cyndi kicked her right leg out to the side as far as she could.

The inside of her ankle snagged the thick cable. "I got it!" Cyndi dragged the cable along the wall with her foot as she returned to the center of the arc.

Lance stopped swinging her and breathed a sigh of relief.

She released her grip on Lance's wrist with her right hand and snatched the cable. "When I say, let go of my left arm."

"Roger that."

Cyndi took a deep, calming breath. She looked up at Lance for encouragement before committing to the perilous next step.

His deep brown eyes were gazing down at her. "You can do this. If you can handle teaching judo to a bunch of bratty little kids, this will be a piece of cake." He looked back over his shoulder then turned back. "Don't forget to swing the cable over to me when you get to the bottom."

"Rocko will be slobbering all over you very soon." She winked. "You have my word." Cyndi took a deep breath then said, "Now!"

Lance let go.

Cyndi disappeared into the fog as she swung away.

The rubber sheath on the outside of the cable had become slippery from the damp fog. Before Cyndi could grab hold with her other hand, she began to drop. She latched on to the cable with both hands and gripped it with all her might. It did little good. She plunged down the side of the silo, clasping the slick cable.

Suddenly, her body jerked to a stop. Her hands had slammed into the metal receptacle at the end of the cable. Excruciating pain radiated up through her arms. Her cries were swallowed up by the fog. The natural reaction would have been to let go of the cable to stop the agony. Cyndi gritted her teeth and forced herself to hold on.

Suspended in the fog, Cyndi had no idea how far she'd fallen.

"Hurry, Pierce is getting closer," Lance yelled out from above.

Cyndi might have been the combat commander in the LCC, but gravity was calling the shots now. She bent her knees slightly to help absorb the impact.

Then she let go.

# CHAPTER 36

CYNDI LANDED ON a steel grate five feet below the end of the umbilical cable. She straightened up and looked around. A catwalk encircled the bottom of the silo. When Cyndi turned around, her mouth dropped open. She was three feet away from the bell-shaped exhaust nozzle protruding from the bottom of the missile's first stage. She reached out and tapped it with her knuckle. It gave off a solid thud.

If the missile had lit off, the searing exhaust blasting out of the nozzle would be powerful enough to launch the massive missile into space at over 15,000 miles per hour.

She grabbed the catwalk railing and tilted her gaze upward. Sixty feet above, obscured by the thick fog, was the business end of the Minuteman. She shivered at the thought that ten live nuclear warheads were sitting right above her with no one controlling them.

Cyndi's hands slipped slightly on the railing. She pulled them away and looked down. Blood dripped from both hands where the sharp edges of the receptacle had sliced into her flesh.

"Are you okay?" Lance yelled out from above.

She wiped her hands on her flight suit. "I'm good. It's only a five-foot drop."

"Swing the cable over. Pierce is getting closer."

Cyndi grabbed the bloody receptacle and slid the cable along the silo wall.

"Got it!" Lance said.

"It's slippery. Grab the cable with both hands and wrap your legs around it. You'll know when you reach the bottom. There's an attachment receptacle at the end."

BAM! BAM!

Shots rang out from above.

The cable swung away.

"Lance!"

Cyndi turned an ear upward.

He didn't respond.

She cautiously crept over to the same spot she'd dropped onto the catwalk and looked up.

The end of the cable swung back and forth.

"Lance! Are you—"

Suddenly, bullets ricocheted off the metal grate.

Cyndi turned and sprinted along the catwalk, dodging to avoid the projectiles.

Gunshots reverberated off the silo walls, making it impossible to track where the shots were coming from. Being trapped inside a dense fog only made the situation worse.

Cyndi squinted, trying to see through the fog while she ran. As she looked back, Cyndi slammed into something, sending her crashing to the metal grate. The abrupt impact had left her dazed and lying flat on her back. Cyndi blinked rapidly and shook her head, trying to regain her senses.

A large figure loomed over her in the mist.

He extended his right arm and pointed it at her.

Cyndi launched her left foot upward, aiming for his kidney.

He snatched her foot, twisted it, and knelt into the back of her knee joint.

Cyndi rolled over to prevent her ankle from snapping.

Her right foot swung across in an arc, striking him in the head. His grip loosened.

Cyndi yanked her foot away and jumped up into the

defensive position.

Lance was standing on the catwalk, holding the side of his head.

"At ease, killer. It's just me," he groaned.

"You scared the crap out of me," Cyndi shot back. "Why didn't you say something?"

He put one finger up to his lips and looked back over his shoulder. Whispering, he said, "In case you forgot, a psycho assassin is coming for us. He can't see us, but he sure as hell can *hear* us. Let's not make it any easier for him." Lance rolled his head in circles to help shake off the painful foot strike. "I slid down the cable just before he grabbed me. Then I ran like hell."

Cyndi gently laid her hand on his temple. "Sorry I kicked you in the head. I thought you were Pierce."

Lance winced at her touch. "The way today is going, a concussion is the least of my worries." He reached up and moved her hand away. Lance felt a warm liquid on his palm. He turned it over and gasped. "You cracked my skull open!"

Cyndi raised both of her bloody hands. "It's not you; it's me."

A shot rang out.

A 9 mm slug slammed into the silo wall behind them, sending concrete chips flying.

They crouched down to minimize their profile.

"Pierce is tall enough to reach the cable," Cyndi said quietly. "It won't be long before he figures out how to get down here."

"We're trapped. All we've done is delay the inevitable." Lance looked around, desperately searching for a way to escape their impending demise. He looked up in awe. "Jesus…" His heart was in his throat.

He was one of the few people on earth who could launch a nuclear missile. But security restrictions had never allowed him to be anywhere near one after being loaded with live warheads.

Standing next to a fully loaded and armed Minuteman IV missile sent a chill down his spine.

Years of training, testing, evaluations, and practice launches at a REACT console simulator had always lacked something. There was an undeniable disconnect. It wasn't "real." Training didn't cause the end of civilization. Practice launches didn't kill millions.

Missileers went to sleep each night comforted by the knowledge that the doctrine of mutually assured destruction had worked so far, and that each side had far too much to lose by starting a nuclear fist fight.

The passing of time had proved the strategy to be legitimate, despite the harsh realities underpinning it.

Cyndi scrutinized the pit below the missile. She cocked her head. Her crystal-blue eyes narrowed. "I think I know a way out of here."

# CHAPTER 37

THE CONCRETE FLAME pit beneath the missile was divided down the middle by a ridge. Each half dipped down then swooped back up at the sides. The concrete ramped up to large metal doors on opposite sides of the silo, placed at the same level as the catwalk. Huge springs attached to the top of the doors pulled them up tracks mounted on the walls when the time came.

"The flames from the rocket motor are redirected up the exhaust diverter tunnels so the missile won't destroy itself before it leaves the silo," Cyndi said, pointing into the pit.

Lance tapped his forehead and nodded. "So, we open one of the diverter tunnel doors, climb up the shaft, and get the hell out of this nightmare."

"Bingo," she replied with obvious pride.

"Nice going, Commander Stafford." Lance leaned in for a kiss.

Cyndi put her hand on his lips. "Save it until we're topside." She pointed to her right. "First, we have to figure out how to open the door."

The reinforced steel door was the size of a one-car garage door and weighed half a ton.

Cyndi and Lance stayed in a low crouch as they went over to the door. They split up, looking for a way to open it.

Lance ran his hand along the bottom edge of it. He

found a latch resembling a large metal claw attached to the door. Metal conduit led away from the latch and into a junction box on the wall. Conduit from the opposite door wrapped around the silo wall and entered the same junction box.

"I think I found something," Lance whispered.

Cyndi joined him.

"See this latch? It looks like it's spring loaded. It must be held in place by an electric coil magnet." He tapped on the junction box. "Cut the power and the latch will retract."

"Very impressive, Deputy Garcia," Cyndi said, smiling broadly.

Lance grabbed the conduit leading from the door latch to the junction box and yanked. When it wouldn't budge, he put a foot on the wall for leverage and yanked again. It stayed solidly attached to the wall.

The new silo would have been destroyed during a launch, but construction crews had built it like it was going to be reloaded and used several times.

When government money was poured into a vital project like nuclear weapons, logic rarely entered the picture.

Lance spotted a fire ax inside a red box on the wall. He scampered over to it.

The words *FOR EMERGENCY USE* ONLY were stenciled on the glass.

He slammed his elbow against the glass cover. It shattered, slicing his sleeve in the process. Blood seeped out of the new wounds.

Shots ricocheted off the wall next to the box. Breaking the glass had tipped off Pierce to his location.

"You two are already dead! It's just a matter of time!" Pierce shrieked, somewhere in the fog.

His words echoed throughout the silo, making it impossible to tell if he'd discovered the umbilical cable and was creeping toward them or if he was still up in the opening.

Lance grabbed the ax and went back to the junction box. "This ought to do the trick." He ushered Cyndi aside, raised the ax, and chopped down with all his might.

The ax blade just bounced off the box, barely nicking it.

"What the hell is this thing made of?" Lance asked with astonishment. He took a second whack at it, with the same result.

Unnerving laughter echoed off the walls.

"So that's how you got down," Pierce shouted from the opening. "Very resourceful. Don't go anywhere, kids. I'll be there in a minute."

"Crap, he discovered the cable." Lance quickly raised the ax over his head for another try.

Just as he was about to swing, Cyndi grabbed his wrist. "Wait!"

"Are you kidding me?" Lance shrieked. "Pierce is coming!"

He tried to pull his arm away, but Cyndi clamped down even tighter. "The last step in the prelaunch sequence is the diverter tunnel doors opening. It's a fail-safe step built into the software. If they didn't open, the extreme heat would cause the rocket fuel to explode before the missile ever cleared the silo. Radioactive material would be scattered for miles."

Lance's head drooped. He lowered the ax. "If I cut the power to the doors, they'll open. That could be the last step the malfunctioning console was looking for to launch the missile. No wonder it kept repeating the number zero."

"If the motor ignites, this silo becomes a raging crematorium." Cyndi contemplated her grisly observation then shook her head. "But if we *don't* open the doors, Pierce…"

"Yeah, there's *that* to consider. Hell of a choice—we

fry, or we die." Lance put down the ax. He held up one hand. "Rock"—he held up the other and joined them—"meet hard place."

Cyndi slumped back against the wall. She let out a long sigh. "I never thought I'd go out this way." Her eyes moistened. "I pictured myself sitting on the front porch, a kid on each knee, telling them stories about my adventures as a fighter pilot."

She swiped at her tears with both hands. The bloody streaks this created along her ivory cheeks almost looked comical.

Lance tried to wipe away the blood with the end of his sleeve, but he only smeared it even more. With resignation in his voice, Lance said, "Well, pumpkin, what's your decision? Cut the power or take our chances with Pierce?"

Cyndi's eyes opened wide. "What did you call me?"

"Pumpkin. Is there a problem?"

Her mother's grating voice popped into Cyndi's head. *Don't worry about me. You do what's best for you.*

She poked Lance in the chest. "Don't ever call me pumpkin again." Cyndi pushed herself away from the wall. "I've made my decision. Make a spare key. I'm moving in." She embraced Lance and planted a passionate kiss on his lips. When they parted, she said, "Cut the power."

Lance saluted. "Yes, ma'am, Captain ma'am."

He picked up the ax.

Cyndi stood next to him as they faced the junction box.

As Lance lifted the ax over his head, he felt the cold steel of a gun barrel press against the back of his neck.

"Not so fast, lover boy."

# CHAPTER 38

"DROP THE AX, Garcia."

Major Pierce had Cyndi's neck in the grasp of his left hand and his Glock pressed up against Lance's spinal column, right below the brain stem.

The ax fell to the catwalk with a loud clang.

"On your knees. Hands on your head," he ordered.

Lance spread his feet and balled up his fists.

"Don't even think about it," Pierce said. He jammed the barrel into Lance's neck even harder. "You'd be dead before either of us could blink."

Lance raised his hands in surrender and knelt on the catwalk. He clasped his hands and rested them on top of his head.

Pierce shoved Cyndi away from Lance and pressed the gun against her temple. He spun her around and slammed her back against the wall. Rage mixed with a look of insanity burned in his eyes as he considered his next move.

Cyndi glowered at Pierce with an intensity she'd never felt before. Every fiber in her body burned with hatred for the man. She spat out the most crushing thing a Special Forces operator could ever hear. "You failed, Pierce!"

"Bullshit! I don't lose. After I kill you and your pathetic boyfriend, I'm going to ride up the elevator and go back to the base. When I tell them I stopped you from launching the missile, I'll be the hero who saved the world from Armageddon while you take the blame for this whole fiasco."

"Hero? Don't flatter yourself. You can lie to yourself all you want. We know the truth. You're just a different variety of evil."

Pierce ignored her stinging observation. "All the eligible guys out there in this big world, and a hot babe like you isn't married?" he observed, nodding at her bare ring finger. "What's the matter, some jerk break your tender heart, sweet cheeks? Or are you just afraid of commitment?"

His cruel comment hit Cyndi like a roundhouse kick to the gut. I'm not afraid to commit, Cyndi told herself. You have it all wrong. The number of fish in the sea is irrelevant. The few men out there who could measure up to my high standards are exceedingly rare, that's all.

"Don't call me sweet cheeks. I hate that name." Cyndi spit in his face.

Pierce wiped away the spittle and sneered. "You're a fighter. I like my women to have a little spunk. After I kill pretty boy over there, I'll show you what a real man can do."

Lance looked up at Pierce and cleared his throat. "Um…that's probably a bad idea."

"Shut up!" Pierce pointed his pistol at Lance's head.

Lance raised his hands. "I'm just warning you; Cyndi gets very upset when men try to force themselves on her. You might want to reconsider."

"Thanks for the advice, dead man. I'll take it from here."

"He's right," Cyndi rejoined. "You lay a hand on me, and I'll teach you the hard way the manners your parents should have taught you."

Cyndi had no idea the danger her words had just unleashed.

Painful memories jolted to the forefront of Pierce's consciousness. Growing up an orphan had left deep scars on his psyche that would never heal. His rage boiled over.

Pierce abandoned the calculating and careful tactics he normally used when dispatching his targets.

Keeping his pistol aimed at Cyndi, Pierce kicked Lance in the ribs, sending him sprawling out on the grate. He grabbed Cyndi by the throat.

She slammed her left knee into his groin.

Pierce barely reacted to the normally debilitating strike. Cyndi didn't know that operators wore cups when going into battle.

He raised his gun, preparing to crush Cyndi's skull with the downward blow.

Before he could strike her, she head-butted Pierce. A sickening cracking sound told Cyndi she'd broken his nose.

Blood gushed down his face. Tears flooded his eyes as Pierce stumbled backward.

Cyndi took advantage of his momentum. She launched herself forward from the wall, jumped up, drew back her knee, and with every ounce of strength she had, slammed the soul of her boot into the center of Pierce's chest.

The strike catapulted Pierce backward into the catwalk railing. When he hit it, he flipped over the metal railing and tumbled into the flame pit.

Cyndi bent over and rested her hands on her knees. "Damn, that hurt," she said, wincing in pain. She closed her eyes and gently rubbed her bruised forehead. With no time to waste trying to sooth her self-inflicted head-ache, Cyndi went over to Lance and helped him to his feet. "Come on; we need to go. Can you swing the ax?"

Lance lightly patted his side, assessing the damage done by Pierce. Searing pain shot through his rib cage. "I don't think so. He broke a few ribs." Lance looked around. "Where is Pierce?"

Cyndi pointed toward the flame pit.

Lance went over to the railing and peered into the pit. Pierce was sprawled out on the concrete. He snickered and said, "I warned you." He went back to the junction box and tried to lift the ax. Lance groaned in pain as the ax slipped from his grip.

"I got this." The fight with Pierce had sent Cyndi's adrenal glands into overdrive. Adrenaline coursed through her veins, giving her superhuman strength. She grabbed the ax, gave Lance a peck on the cheek, and landed a devastating blow on the junction box.

# CHAPTER 39

SPARKS SHOT OUT of the box as the wires shorted out.

The heavy doors rocketed up their rails.

Cyndi and Lance closed their eyes, clutched each other tightly, and waited for the inevitable.

Seconds ticked away.

They cracked opened their eyelids to sneak a peek at the missile.

The fact that they were still alive took a few moments to register in their brains.

When it finally did, they jumped up and down, still clutching each other.

"You did it!" Lance shouted, ignoring his pain. He turned to look at the diverter tunnel.

A six-foot-wide opening in the wall had appeared. Beautiful, golden beams of sunlight lit up their path to safety. The nightmare was over. Soon, they would be above ground again.

They rushed to the opening.

"You first," Cyndi said, pointing up the tunnel.

Lance shook his head. "No. I'll follow you."

"You're injured. If you need help, I'll be right behind you."

Before Lance could object, Cyndi planted her hands on her hips and barked, "That's an order."

After all that had happened that day, Lance knew better than to get into a contest of wills with Cyndi. "Okay, I'll go first."

Before he started up the tunnel, they heard a loud moan coming from the direction of the flame pit.

"He's still alive," Lance said.

"I'll see you in hell, sweet cheeks!" Pierce wailed from the pit.

Gunfire erupted from below.

Cyndi and Lance ducked down and pressed themselves into the opening.

Oddly, the bullets weren't hitting anywhere near them.

Cyndi looked over at the missile. Pierce was firing at the first-stage fuel tank.

"That lunatic is trying to detonate the solid rocket fuel!" she shrieked in horror. "Go! Go!"

Rungs had been built into the wall of the diverter tunnel to allow maintenance crews to crawl through it when they inspected the concrete for cracks.

Lance grabbed the first rung and scampered up the tunnel.

Cyndi was right behind him. She couldn't help having the dispiriting thought of making it this far only to be incinerated just as they reached the top of the tunnel. "Faster!"

Lance got to the top of the tunnel and poked his head above ground. Bright sunlight forced him to shield his eyes and turn away. He took in a deep, satisfying breath of the fresh Wyoming air.

The opening above the missile was to his left, only four feet away. Lance leaned over the opening. He could see the tip of the Minuteman missile. It was made from an exotic material that could survive the searing heat generated by traveling at hypersonic speeds through the thick atmosphere.

Lance climbed out and reached back down into the tunnel to lend Cyndi a hand. Once she was topside, Lance cupped his hands around his mouth and yelled back down the tunnel. "Take that, Rambo! A couple of missileers just beat you at your own game. It's over. You lost!"

Lance planted his hands on his hips and surveyed the site with a triumphant smirk.

His celebration of beating Pierce was short lived.

A frown formed on his face. "Shit."

Thirty-mile-an-hour winds had dropped the wind-chill to a perilous minus twenty degrees. Bitterly cold air slapped Lance's face like a scorned wife. His exhalations instantly crystalized after blowing past his chattering teeth.

By design, the site was located miles from civilization. Gently rolling countryside, covered in deep snow, stretched out before him. Not one single building was in sight. Cows that normally roamed the verdant pasturelands had been safely tucked away in warm barns.

The thin Nomex flight suits they were wearing were no match for a Wyoming winter. Their bodies shivered uncontrollably. Without parkas or gloves, severe hypothermia would set in long before they could reach the nearest farmhouse.

The wide-open spaces prized by those hardy souls still infused with the pioneering spirit—and that Cyndi had grown to like—had now become a lethal enemy.

What the skilled Delta Force team had failed to do, Mother Nature would accomplish in only fifteen minutes.

# CHAPTER 40

CYNDI BRIEFLY CONSIDERED climbing back down into the warm silo to escape the deadly low temperature. Knowing that Pierce was still alive quickly eliminated that option. She looked over at the building they'd entered when they arrived at Alpha One. It was in shambles. The C-4 had blown out the front of the building and collapsed the roof. Taking shelter in the ruins of the building would shield them somewhat from the wind but not the subzero temperature.

And they would still be nearby a malfunctioning Minuteman IV missile that might explode or launch at any moment.

"We've got to find a way to get back to base and get a crisis response crew out here," Cyndi said.

"Maybe we could hitchhike." Lance looked for the country road that ran parallel to the site. Two feet of undisturbed snow made it impossible to distinguish it from the grassland.

Cyndi rotated around, searching for a solution. She froze.

A pair of AH-6M Little Bird helicopters sat quietly on the helipad outside the perimeter fence.

Without saying a word, she sprinted through the snow and toward the breach in the fence.

Lance did his best to keep up with her.

Cyndi lay on her back and pushed herself under the fence with the heels of her boots. Once her top half was outside the fence, she sat up and scooted backward until her feet cleared.

Lance lay on his back and imitated her move. Halfway through the opening, his flight suit got caught on a jagged barb. He reached back over his head. "I'm stuck. Pull me."

Cyndi grabbed his hands and yanked.

The barb ripped open his flight suit. He pulled the fabric free and got on his feet outside the fence.

They raced over to the nearest helicopter and climbed into the cockpit. Cyndi took the right seat while Lance took the left.

Doors were a luxury most small military helicopters lacked. Weight saved by not having doors could be put into more bullets, rockets, and high-tech avionics.

With only a partial reprieve from the howling wind, Lance asked, "Now what? I don't know how to fly one of these."

"I do." Cyndi felt the need to qualify her surprising statement. "Well, I used to. It's been years since my dad taught me to fly helicopters at the flight school."

"It'll come back to you. It's just like riding a bicycle, right?" Lance said hopefully.

Cyndi rolled her eyes at his naively optimistic comment. She scanned the instrument panel looking for anything familiar. "I've never flown something this modern."

Special Operation forces were always first in line at getting the latest technology upgrades before the rest of the grunts in the military.

The center pedestal between the seats was loaded with radios and electronics. The pedestal extended forward then up, splitting the bubble canopy. Large glass cockpit displays, and a plethora of buttons and switches, filled the space. Everything a trained pilot needed to successfully carry out their mission was there.

Cyndi had learned to fly helicopters in an antiquated

trainer years ago. She had no idea where to start to get this bird flyable. She carefully scanned the cockpit, reading the labels next to each switch and button. Slowly, she began to make sense out of the futuristic cockpit.

First, she turned on the battery. The screens flickered then displayed the flight instruments. Next, she engaged the starter, fuel, and ignition. The Rolls-Royce turboshaft engine coughed to life. The rotors began to spin. Thirty seconds later the helicopter was ready for flight.

Cyndi didn't even bother trying to figure out the complex navigation systems. All aircraft are required to have an old-fashioned magnetic compass installed, regardless of the fancy avionics on board. She knew the base was west of their location. Cyndi checked her watch. The afternoon sun in the southwest sky, combined with the trusty compass, would be enough to get them headed in the right direction. Hopefully, they would end up somewhere in the vicinity of Cheyenne. If Cyndi flew high enough, picking out the city from the snow-covered prairie should be easy. Using her knowledge of the roads in town, she could then steer the helicopter toward Warren AFB.

She nudged Lance. "I'm going to have my hands full trying to fly this thing. I need you to be my copilot. Can you do it?"

"Absolutely," Lance shot back with a confident grin on his face. "I didn't watch *Top Gun* twenty-seven times for volleyball tips. I've wanted to be a pilot ever since I joined the Air Force." He looked like a kid eagerly waiting to open his first Christmas present. Lance couldn't contain himself. He started pushing buttons and flipping switches.

"Okay, Ice Man, take it easy. Put on your headset. I'll tell you what I want you to do."

They donned their headsets and did a check of the intercom.

Lance saluted Cyndi. "Ready for takeoff, Captain. Fly this thing like you stole it!"

"Hang on to something," Cyndi warned.

She brought the engine up to full speed. Cyndi gradually pulled up on the collective. The weight on the skids lessened, then they broke ground. Strong winds caused the craft to drift perilously close to the other helicopter. Cyndi overreacted, yanking the cyclic left. The helicopter tilted sideways, bringing the tips of the rotors perilously close to the ground. She overcorrected again, this time causing the craft to bounce up and down on the helipad like a novice on a pogo stick.

Lance latched on to the doorframe with a death grip to keep from being tossed out.

Cyndi cut the power to settle the helicopter down on the pad—and the butterflies in her stomach.

They both grabbed their seat belts and strapped in tightly.

Cyndi increased power and lifted off again. The aircraft wobbled around in the sky but steadily gained altitude. Once they'd reached five hundred feet, she nudged the helicopter forward and headed west.

They were so overjoyed to be going home, the frigid air swirling around in the open cockpit didn't bother them in the least.

"The nightmare is over. We did it," Lance said jubilantly as he fist-bumped Cyndi. "If I never see another Minuteman missile again, it'll be too soon."

Cyndi took one final look back at Alpha One. Her sterling record as a missileer had earned her the honor of being chosen the first commander of the new site by General McNeil. She had been expected to represent all missileers and the Global Strike Command in its mission to provide America with a safe, secure, and lethal nuclear option.

She thought about her duty as a missileer, shook her

head, and let out a heavy sigh. "We can't leave."

Lance jerked back. "What?"

"We have to go back."

"Are you crazy?"

"Ten live nuclear warheads are sitting out in the open on an unsecured Minuteman missile. Anyone driving by could see that. If that gets out on social media, the whole world will know. Including the bad guys."

Lance nodded knowingly. "You're right. Regardless of what happens next, we're still missileers. We never compromise the security of a nuclear weapon."

"We have to destroy any possible access to the missile."

"How?"

Cyndi pointed. "Look out your door."

# CHAPTER 41

TWO HELLFIRE MISSILES hung off the left pylon. "An intruder could easily get through the opening in the fence and take the elevator down or get to the warheads from above," Cyndi said. "We have to eliminate both options before we leave."

Cyndi swung the helicopter around to the east. The sun was at her back, providing perfect conditions to attack the site.

"I'll get us set up for a shot, you figure out how to launch the missiles," she instructed Lance.

"Time out," Lance said loudly. "You want me to shoot a missile…at a thermonuclear missile? In case you missed that part in missileer school, those things make one hell of a big bang."

"I'm not going to aim for the missile, I'm going to aim for the ground *around* the silo. The explosion should rain so much dirt down on the opening, it would be impossible to get to the warheads. I'll take out the building next, cutting off access by the elevator."

Lance crossed his arms defiantly. "After *that* takeoff, you want me to believe you can steer this helicopter so precisely that the missile will hit the ground *next to* the silo?"

Cyndi took her hands off the controls. "You want to do it?"

"Touché," Lance replied sheepishly, with his hands raised in surrender. "You fly. I'll figure out how to fire the missiles." He searched the instrument panel for the right switches.

"I don't have to aim the helicopter; the missiles are laser guided. Put the crosshairs next to the silo, and the missile will do the rest."

Lance turned on the laser designator. Then he powered up the forward-looking infrared camera under the chin of the helicopter. A black-and-white view of the site popped up on one of the cockpit screens. The infrared camera didn't actually *see* the scene ahead. It translated minute differences in the temperature of objects into pictures.

Through trial and error, Lance figured out how to move the crosshairs. He placed them ten feet away from the silo opening.

Cyndi put the helicopter in a shallow dive, doing her best to keep it steady in the gusty winds. "Okay, get ready. When I say, squeeze the trigger on your stick."

Lance pointed at the screen. "There's a problem."

A glowing white blob in the shape of a man, was running across the grounds.

Cyndi shook her head in disgust. "Crap, it's Pierce."

This unexpected news forced Cyndi and Lance to focus even more sharply on their tasks.

"Cleared to arm the missile," Cyndi said.

"Master arm switch on."

He held the crosshairs right on target while Cyndi made final adjustments to their flight path.

"Now!"

Lance squeezed the trigger.

The Hellfire missile roared off the rail.

The white blob on the screen stopped moving, then immediately started running perpendicular to the path of the missile.

The guidance system in the nose of the missile locked on to the spot where the laser reflected off the ground. It hit exactly where Lance had aimed it.

Cyndi pulled up and passed over the silo. When she looked back, a small cloud of dust billowed up from the site, but the nose cone of the Minuteman IV was still clearly visible.

The apron around the silo was covered in concrete that was four feet thick. It needed to be that deep to support the weight of the massive truck that had transported the new missile to the site.

The aptly named Transporter Erector Loader truck weighed over 107,000 pounds with a missile inside its custom-built trailer. Every foot of the dirt road leading to the site, all the way back to the highway, had to be torn up and replaced with high-strength concrete to support the thirty-two wheels on the enormous truck. All courtesy of Uncle Sam.

The TEL driver would back his truck up to the silo, raise the missile up vertically, then try to carefully lower the rocket into the silo without accidentally banging it into the wall. The job felt like playing the classic kid's game Operation but with much graver consequences for failure than a red light and buzzer.

The Hellfire missile had done a bang-up job splintering the thick concrete apron, but that's all.

"Only one missile left," Lance said, stating the obvious.

Cyndi faced a crucial decision: destroy the remainder of the building and access to the elevator with the last missile or take a second shot at the ground next to the silo, hoping to bury the missile in debris.

Instead of concern, a confident look suddenly spread across her face. She hadn't put in hundreds of hours studying for the weekly readiness tests for nothing.

She pulled the helicopter up into a steep climb. Just as the craft stalled out, she stomped on the right anti-torque pedal. The AH-6M performed an acrobatic pirouette in the sky, spinning 180 degrees. With the nose now pointed straight down, it rapidly gained airspeed. Cyndi smoothly pulled out of the dive and set up for another pass. She tapped the picture on the screen and smiled. "Put the crosshairs right here."

# CHAPTER 42

"THAT SHOULD *DEFINITELY* do the trick," Lance replied, with an equally big smile.

He slewed the crosshairs over a large metal cylinder behind the building. Two thousand gallons of diesel fuel was stored in the tank. The fuel was used to power generators on site in the event the local electric grid went down.

The destructive power of the high-explosive warhead on the Hellfire missile would be multiplied a hundred times by the exploding fuel.

Now it was up to the laws of physics to determine if that would be enough to cut off both paths to the warheads.

As Lance adjusted the crosshairs on the screen, he could see the glowing outline of Major Pierce huddled against the fence. His warm body stood out like a beacon against the snowy terrain. Bright white flashes were seen coming from his outstretched hand. In a last-ditch attempt to get revenge, he was firing his Glock at the helicopter as it set up for its run. The small bullets went harmlessly wide or bounced off the solidly built attack helicopter.

Lance placed the crosshairs over the center of the fuel tank.

"Missile armed, waiting for your command."

Cyndi shut out every distraction around her. She concentrated on flying a glidepath as perfectly focused as the laser that illuminated the fuel tank.

"Fire!"

The Hellfire missile streaked toward the tank at over one thousand miles per hour. Halfway to its target, the missile suddenly lurched upward. Its guidance system computer had mistaken the thick-walled fuel tank for a T-90 Russian tank.

As the missile crossed over the fence it pitched sharply down and struck the fuel tank from directly overhead—the same way it would attack the relatively vulnerable turret on the top of a tank.

Alpha One erupted.

A huge mushroom cloud of boiling fire shot into the air.

Cyndi banked hard right to avoid being consumed by the fireball. The shock wave punched the small helicopter like it had been hit by the hand of God.

"Jesus Christ!" Lance bellowed.

The fact that he was still in one piece—and able to shout out such an apropos exclamation—told him the warheads had not detonated.

Wood, steel, dirt, and concrete were hurled hundreds of feet into the air. It rained down on the open silo, burying the missile.

Where the building had once stood, a smoldering twenty-foot-deep crater was all that was left. As ravaged as the scene was, Cyndi couldn't help but think how it would have looked if the warheads had exploded.

"Nice shootin', Tex," Cyndi said with a twinkle in her eye. "Let's go find General McNeil."

Using her best guess, she steered the helicopter on a westerly heading and hoped that it would be sufficient to get them safely back to the base. She climbed to five thousand feet to make it easier to spot Cheyenne.

The Little Bird helicopter flew serenely along in the smooth air. Cyndi found the controls for the heater and cranked it up to its maximum setting.

Now that she was able to warm up a little, her thoughts shifted to how they could possibly explain everything that had happened at Alpha One to her boss. Odds were low that he'd be thrilled to hear their story. McNeil would immediately order a team to Alpha One to secure the site and the missile. Then a reckoning would be coming.

"Since we have time, we need to talk about how we're going to break the bad news to the general," Cyndi said.

"We?" Lance said with mock surprise. "You're the crew commander. I'm just a lowly deputy. You didn't actually think I was serious back there when I said we're in this together." The goofy smirk on his face told Cyndi he was attempting to be humorous.

"If you're that worried about McNeil's reaction, feel free to get out at any time," Cyndi replied, pointing at the open door next to Lance.

"No thanks. I'll stay and take my chances," he said.

Cyndi searched the horizon for any sign of the city. All she saw was an endless expanse of featureless white prairie. She leaned forward and squinted, looking for any recognizable landmarks. Off to her eleven o'clock something caught her eye. A long ribbon of concrete stretched from horizon to horizon. Interstate 80 ran parallel to their flight path. The highway would serve as their guide, leading them directly into Cheyenne.

Pioneers making their way west in covered wagons could never have imagined such a smooth, effortless path to follow on their journey to a new life.

Cyndi turned on the autopilot and sat back in her seat. The tension in her body began to recede. Her shoulders relaxed.

Suddenly, the large plexiglass bubble canopy surrounding the cockpit shattered.

# CHAPTER 43

THE CANOPY SPLINTERED into a spiderweb of cracks. Luckily, it was designed to take battle damage but stay intact.

Cyndi immediately slowed the helicopter to lessen the force of the wind on the windscreen, hoping to prevent it from caving in on them. She scanned the outside of the canopy for the guts of a bird, assuming a bird strike. It was clean. She looked closer. There was one small hole in the center of the glass.

Cyndi stuck her head out the side door and looked back. A thousand yards behind, the second AH-6M was bearing down on them. Muzzle flashes coming from the Gatling gun looked like a strobe light.

"Pierce!" Cyndi screamed.

She slammed the stick to the right. The copter snapped into a violent turn. It dropped out of the sky like a very expensive rock. Airspeed quickly jumped past redline. The damaged canopy began to flex inward.

Pierce mimicked Cyndi's maneuver, staying right on her tail.

Tracers whizzed by the cockpit.

A shrill tone suddenly went off in their headsets. The missile warning system was telling them they'd been locked on to by a heat seeking missile.

"Flares!"

Lance frantically searched the instrument panel for the switch to deploy the flares to break the missile's lock before it was too late. He found it.

A staccato of white-hot flares spewed out of each side of the rear fuselage until the flare canisters were empty. They arced across the sky then looped downward.

The seeker head on the missile broke its lock. The warning tone stopped.

Cyndi put the helicopter into a dive then leveled off a few feet above the ground, hoping to prevent another lock-on. Cottonwood trees and sagebrush rushed by in a blur. A rooster tail of snowflakes shot up into the air behind the helicopter.

Bullets from Pierce's Gatling gun stitched a line across the snow off to their left.

"Do something!"

"I can't outrun him; the windscreen might collapse on us," Cyndi warned.

She looked back. Pierce was closing in.

The turboshaft engine suddenly went from a roar to a purr.

"What are you doing?" Lance gasped.

Cyndi had chopped the power to idle.

She was far too busy trying to avoid being shot out of the sky to spell out her plan. Cyndi put the helicopter into a series of S turns over the highway, making it impossible for Pierce to get off a clear shot at his distance. The gap between the two aircraft quickly closed. Pierce was now only one football field length behind them.

He slewed the Gatling gun straight ahead and waited for his prey to cross in front of him.

Lance looked back and yelled, "He's going to fire!"

"Wait...wait..." Cyndi said calmly.

When Lance turned around, he jolted back in his seat. "Holy shit!"

A highway overpass loomed directly in front of them. Cyndi kept the helicopter inches above Interstate 80. Showers of sparks trailed behind them as the skids occasionally skipped off the concrete.

Barreling toward the reinforced concrete overpass at over ninety miles per hour, the bright yellow sign mounted on it was clearly visible: *16' CLEARANCE.*

When he saw what she was doing, Pierce's eyes bulged out. He debated following Cyndi on her suicidal maneuver. Uncharacteristic doubt shoved aside his normal approach of reckless abandon. Pierce hesitated for a moment then yanked back on the cyclic. His helicopter zoomed up into a steep climbing right turn away from the overpass. He did a full circle, looping back around to the highway. Pierce slowed to a hover and searched the road for the wreckage. The charred bodies of Cyndi and Lance were nowhere to be found. Pierce climbed up five hundred feet to get a better view.

Off in the distance, clouds of snow were being kicked up by semi-trucks swerving off the highway onto the shoulder.

———◆———

Lance's face was ashen. He looked like he was going to throw up. The crazy maneuver had shaken him up so badly he couldn't think of a joke to mask his fear. "You know I wasn't being literal about flying like you stole it, right?"

"Relax; we lost him, didn't we?" Cyndi said with a wry grin. "Congratulations, Ice Man, you just earned your copilot wings." She gave him a playful punch on the arm.

Cyndi kept the helicopter skimming along right above the highway. Trucks and cars swerved off the road and into the ditch after seeing a menacing attack helicopter roaring up behind them in their rearview mirrors.

Cyndi decided to take pity on the startled motorists and climbed to a more reasonable altitude. Slowly, the bustling metropolis of Cheyenne, Wyoming, came into view. Built from Wyoming sandstone, the Renaissance revival-style state capitol building stood out from the surrounding structures. The afternoon sun reflected off its 24-karat gold leaf dome, acting like a beacon welcoming them home.

"We need clearance from Cheyenne tower to enter their airspace and land at Warren," Cyndi informed Lance. She tapped on a piece of equipment in the center pedestal. "This is the radio. I have no idea what the tower frequency is. Dial in one two one point five, the universal emergency frequency. All air traffic control facilities are required to monitor it."

Lance set up the frequency.

Cyndi pressed the mic button on her stick. "Cheyenne tower, this is…uh…" It suddenly occurred to her that she didn't know the call sign of the helicopter. "This is Capt. Cyndi Stafford. I am about ten miles east, requesting permission to land at F. E. Warren."

"Say your call sign," the controller replied, annoyance evident in his voice.

"I don't know my call sign."

"Say your aircraft type, then."

"Helicopter."

"Care to elaborate?" the controller said sarcastically.

"I think it's called a Little Bird," Cyndi replied, guessing. "Let's just say my callsign is Alpha One. Requesting permission to enter your airspace and get vectors directly to Warren Air Force Base."

"So, you don't know your call sign, and you don't know what aircraft you're sitting in. I'm going to go out on a limb here, but I'm guessing you don't have a flight plan either," he rudely replied.

Cyndi felt like unloading on the snarky controller but bit her tongue. "Look, we've had a really rough day. All I want to do is get this over with. I know you have your rules, but if you'd just clear us into your airspace, I'd appreciate it."

"And *I'd* appreciate it if you followed the federal aviation regulations," he shot back. "Only aircraft that have filed a flight plan and are on official business are authorized to land at the base."

Cyndi played her aviation ace in the hole. "Alpha One declaring an emergency. I need a heading direct to Warren right now."

The veteran controller mashed the mic button. "Nice try, little birdie, clearance denied. Call back after you've filed a flight plan. The same goes for your wingman. Over and out."

Cyndi turned toward Lance. Her brow furrowed. "My wingman?"

The missile warning system let out a shrill, pulsating tone.

Cyndi instinctively jinked left, then right. Precious seconds ticked by as the helicopter darted through the sky performing defensive maneuvers. Cyndi looked over her shoulder, searching for the telltale white smoke trail of an air-to-air missile. She spied a black dot at the same altitude in the distance. "Pierce just locked on to us, but he must be outside firing range." Cyndi pushed the helicopter up to its maximum speed. The shattered canopy began to vibrate. "Cheyenne Tower, Alpha One is coming through your airspace whether you like it or not. Clear all traffic."

"Permission denied!" the startled controller yelled into his microphone. "I have aircraft about to take off. You are not cleared into my airspace. Acknowledge, Alpha One!"

Cyndi ignored him.

"Alpha One, landing at Warren Air Force Base is restricted. Acknowledge my transmission. Now!"

Two F-16s on their way back to Hill AFB were taxiing to the runway.

The controller decided to enlist their help. "Viper One-Six flight, I've got two unidentified helicopters inbound to Warren Air Force Base without authorization. You are cleared for takeoff. Request that you intercept them and force them to turn away from the base."

The F-16 lead pilot knew of Warren and its nuclear mission. "Happy to help, tower. Whoever these jokers are, they have no business getting anywhere near that base. After we scare them a little, I'm sure they'll have a change of heart."

Cyndi bounced up and down in her seat with excitement as she keyed her mic. "Yes, yes, that's perfect. This is the lead helicopter. Come and intercept us. My wingman is trying to kill us. We need you fighter jocks to protect us and escort us to the base."

The F-16s screeched to a stop just as they began their takeoff roll. The formation leader jumped on the radio. "Tower, what the hell is going on here?"

"Stand by," the controller responded. "Alpha One, repeat your last transmission."

Cyndi could see the field through the cracked canopy. "A psycho is on our tail. He's trying to murder us. If we don't get to the headquarters building on base, an armed nuclear missile could detonate at any moment. Launch the F-16s!"

The leader looked over at his wingman and spun his fingertip in circles next to his head. Over the radio he announced, "Tower, that chick sounds like she's nuts. We're going to sit this one out until I find out what is going on."

The missile warning system activated again. Sharp pulsating tones meant that the Stinger missile on Pierce's left pylon was searching for its victim.

"No, you can't do that! He's going to shoot. Take off, dammit!"

"Viper One-Six flight will be taxiing back to the ramp," the leader calmly said.

Branded a rule follower all her life—as if that were

a bad thing—Cyndi decided it was time to make her own rules. "Sorry, guys, that's not going to happen." She armed the Gatling gun and squeezed off fifty rounds.

# CHAPTER 44

BULLETS TRACED A line across the runway, five feet in front of the formation.

Cyndi knew the fighter pilot personality well. Her provocation had the exact desired effect.

"Lead has the first helicopter; you take the second one! Viper One-Six flight, release breaks. Go to full afterburner. Shoot to kill!"

The F-16s leaped forward with a thunderous roar.

Cyndi put her helicopter into a dive and aimed it at the end of the runway. The missile warning tone stopped pulsating and went solid. She held her heading.

The fighters rapidly gained speed as they rolled down the runway.

A suicidal game of chicken was about to take place.

The Fighting Falcons broke ground and scooped their landing gear up into their bellies. The leader kept the planes on the deck to maximize acceleration.

Cyndi caught site of them at her twelve o'clock and closing fast. She held her heading.

The wingman spread out into tactical position, thirty feet to the leader's right side. The pilots flipped on their AN/APG-68 fire control radars. Antennas in their nose cones swept back and forth sending out radar pulses.

The antennas stopped searching and pointed straight at Cyndi's helicopter.

"Game over, crazy lady." The leader took one last look up from his radar screen before firing. The AH-6M Little

Bird attack helicopter flew right between the two fighters.

The stunned pilots instinctively jerked their planes away from each other.

The lead pilot put his jet into a bone-crushing nine G climb to start a half loop and then double back on Cyndi from above after executing an Immelmann maneuver.

The wingman turned his attention to Pierce's helicopter. Unfortunately, he had failed to notice the missile warning tone in his own headset during all the chaos.

The Stinger missile that Pierce had fired had broken lock with Cyndi's helicopter and latched on to his plane.

Traveling at Mach 2.2, it rapidly closed the gap on the unsuspecting wingman—who was almost supersonic himself—at a combined closure rate of 2,300 miles per hour.

The pilot never had a chance to get off a shot. He yanked back on the stationary fly-by-wire control stick with one hundred pounds of brute force. The missile struck just as he pulled up. The right wing of the Fighting Falcon was blown off by the detonation. Black smoke and bright red flames trailed the plane as it corkscrewed up into the sunny Wyoming sky.

"I'm hit! I'm hit!" the wingman screamed over the radio.

The leader was inverted and just about to roll out of the Immelmann. He looked back over his shoulder and yelled, "Eject! Ej—"

Before he could finish his transmission, his wingman's plane disintegrated. Blazing pieces of fighter aircraft spread gracefully across the sky like a spectacular firework display.

———◆———

Cyndi waved at the controller as they flew past the tower.

After resuming breathing, Lance asked in a shaky voice, "How did you know?"

With Warren now in sight, she turned to her copilot. "My dad loved to talk about practice dogfights he flew against his squadron mates. He would weave his hands back and forth when he talked, replaying the engagements. According to him, he never lost. His favorite tactic was to turn in to his opponents, so that their missiles were inside their minimum firing range. All that deadly firepower became useless."

"With two pissed-off pilots out for blood coming straight at us, you calculated the minimum firing range of their missiles in only a few seconds?" Lance asked incredulously.

"No, not exactly…" Cyndi smiled and shrugged. "I just guessed."

Lance's mouth dropped open.

"Hey, it worked, didn't it?" Cyndi countered in her defense.

———◆———

The panicked tower controller grabbed a phone and dialed the security office on base. When the dispatcher on duty picked up, the controller yelled, "This is Cheyenne airport tower, an unauthorized helicopter is headed for your base. I believe we have a 9/11 scenario in progress. I think the helicopter is going to pull a kamikaze and crash into the headquarters building. Alert all your men. This is not a drill!"

———◆———

"Your ass is mine, you son of a bitch!" The formation leader broke off his attack on Cyndi's helicopter and put his plane into a tight turn to the east. He locked on to Pierce's helicopter and fired off an AIM-9 Sidewinder infrared missile.

Pierce saw the missile launch and deployed flares to draw it away. The missile sailed by his helicopter and chased after one of the flares until it nosedived harmlessly into the ground next to the runway.

The F-16 pilot turned away, setting up for an attack from the rear.

Pierce slammed on the brakes and put his helicopter into a hover. Using the anti-torque pedals to rotate his helicopter, he tracked the fighter like a skeet shooter tracks the clay target as it flies across his view. Pierce mashed his trigger down. The three barrels of the GAU-19 Gatling gun glowed white hot as they spewed out two thousand rounds a minute.

Chunks of lead pierced the jet's engine. Flames and oily black smoke erupted out of the tailpipe. The pilot pulled up into a climb to get his crippled bird as far from terra firma as possible as he assessed the damage and looked for an uninhabited area. To save time, he rested his left hand on the ejection seat handle .

---

Pierce spied Cyndi's helicopter flying over the base. It was slowing down to begin its approach for landing. He slammed the cyclic forward and revved the engine past redline. He quickly closed the distance between the two helicopters and fired the Gatling gun.

---

"I'll land at the base heliport, then we'll go to head-quarters and tell General McNeil what happened," Cyndi informed Lance.

Suddenly, a loud drumbeat of a noise came from over their heads.

Bullets tore through the oil tank in the engine compartment, setting it on fire. Without vital lubrication, the engine instantly seized up.

The instrument panel lit up with flashing red warning lights. The rotors began to slow, robbing the helicopter of precious lift.

Cyndi frantically searched for an open patch of ground to land on before the rotors lost all lift and autorotation became impossible.

---

Pierce swooped in for the kill. Now only half a mile away from the gravely wounded Little Bird, Pierce let out a maniacal laugh. "I never lose, sweet cheeks! See you in hell!"

Hatred, ego, and an ultracompetitive personality had caused him to become so focused on killing Lance and Cyndi that he'd lost all situational awareness. Major Pierce, Delta Force team leader, had violated the number one rule in the Special Operations world—never *assume* your adversary is dead.

An AIM-7 Sparrow missile flew right into the open door of his AH-6M before exploding.

Pierce was dead long before his helicopter fell from the sky and slammed into the parade field on the base.

Cyndi was right about pilots.

Pierce wasn't the only warrior who lived by the motto I Never Lose. The F-16 pilot had turned his fatally damaged jet toward Pierce and fired off the missile just before ejecting.

# CHAPTER 45

CYNDI IGNORED THE fiery explosion off in the distance at the parade field. Her entire focus was on getting them down in one piece. With the engine on fire, she only had one chance to get the autorotation right.

At their low altitude, making it to the heliport was impossible. The headquarters building was dead ahead. It had a large parking lot that was only half-full. Cyndi made a snap decision and committed to landing there.

The crippled helicopter fell from the sky. At the last second, she pulled up on the collective and eased back on the cyclic. The nose pitched up. Cyndi was trying to round out of the rapid descent at the same point that the helicopter would contact the ground—without stalling first. In a helicopter she'd never flown before.

She'd started the flair ten feet too low.

The AH-6M slammed into the pavement.

Its skids splayed outward.

Both pylons snapped off.

The spinning rotors flexed downward on impact. The tips of the composite blades shattered as they sliced through the tail boom. Razor-sharp pieces peppered the headquarters building, shattering windows. Startled office workers dove for cover under their desks..

As designed, the structure under their seats collapsed, absorbing the energy from the hard landing that would have otherwise crushed their spines.

Cyndi and Lance were dazed from the impact. They

sat motionless for a few moments. Slowly, they began to get their wits about them. Sore but thankful to be in one piece, the missileers unbuckled.

"You okay?" Cyndi asked groggily.

Lance rubbed his neck. "I think so." There was an odd sensation on the back of his hand as he massaged his neck. He lowered his hand. The skin on the back was pink and the hair had been singed off. With his senses still caught up in a cloud of confusion, the reason didn't immediately register in his mind.

Lance looked up. The ceiling was engulfed in flames. Fire from the burst oil tank had burned through the roof and was now spreading to the cockpit.

Lance shoved Cyndi out her door then dove out the opening on his side. With the skids collapsed, the fall was only two feet.

They got to their feet and limped away from the burning helicopter, rejoining at the steps leading up to the building.

In seconds, the fire had breached the fuel tank.

The Little Bird detonated with a thunderous BOOM.

Rounds from the Gatling gun began to light off, sounding like popcorn cooking on a stove. Nearby cars were caught up in the conflagration, exploding as well. The parking lot resembled a scene from Dante's *Inferno*.

Cyndi and Lance looked away and shielded their faces from the intense heat. Passersby rushed toward the burning helicopter, ignoring their own safety.

Although terrible, this accident paled in comparison to the destruction that would have happened if their missile had launched or had fallen into the wrong hands. With a renewed sense of urgency, they climbed the concrete steps leading to the headquarters building. The imposing, modern structure was palatial in comparison to most of the other buildings on base.

———◆———

Before leaving the command post, Colonel Wilmer
had threatened his staff with prison time if they told anyone about the incident at Alpha One. He scurried down
the sidewalk leading to the headquarters building with a
death grip on a manila folder. Despite the freezing temperature, he was perspiring. "Why me?" he asked himself
rhetorically. Something caught his eye. He looked up just
as the helicopter slammed into the parking lot. He wad-
dled off toward the lot in a partial jog.

Wilmer approached the flaming wreckage but was
driven back by the severe heat. He decided to direct the
rescue efforts from afar and let braver souls risk injury
searching for survivors.

———◆———

Lance yanked open the heavy, ornate metal door leading into the 90th Missile Wing headquarters building.

Spotless, polished granite covered the expansive lobby.
The Global Strike Command emblem was centered in
the floor. The walls were lined with flags representing
every unit in the command. To the right, a middle-aged
receptionist sat behind a large marble-clad desk. When
Cyndi and Lance rushed up to her, she looked up and let
out a frightful scream.

It was no wonder; they looked like they'd just finished
a shift at the slaughterhouse.

Blood covered Cyndi's hands and was streaked across
her cheeks from wiping her tears away in the silo. Her
flight suit was covered in soot from the burning helicopter.

Lance wouldn't be auditioning for commercials any-
time soon. Blood-soaked gauze was wrapped around his
leg, his elbow was blood-stained, his flight suit was torn,

and he had dried blood on the side of his head where Cyndi had kicked him.

"Oh my God! What happened to you?" the receptionist asked, wide-eyed.

"It's a long story," Lance quipped.

"We have to see General McNeil right now. It's an emergency. Where is his office?" Cyndi pleaded.

"Down that hallway," the woman responded, pointing across the lobby. "But you can't just storm in there! You need an appointment!" She began leafing through her appointment book. "And a bath," she said under her breath.

Cyndi and Lance ignored her snide comment and sprinted across the lobby.

"You need an appointment!" the woman yelled out in vain.

A security policeman stood at the entrance to the hallway. He wore a ceremonial uniform with a sash across his chest made of braided golden cord, a chartreuse wool beret canted off to one side, and patent leather shoes polished to a blinding sheen. He'd heard the encounter with the receptionist and moved to block off the hallway.

"You heard the lady, no one sees the general without an appointment," the guard barked, his hand held out like a stop sign.

At this point in their astonishingly bad day, neither missileer felt like wasting their time getting in a debate with a self-important guard whose most hazardous duty was to defend a hallway.

"You want to take this one, Lieutenant Garcia?" Cyndi asked. "I'm not in the mood to argue with a toy soldier."

Lance looked the guard up and down. "I don't know. Anybody who can get their shoes that shiny is probably pretty tough. Let's flip a coin. Loser has to kick his ass."

Cyndi patted the sides of her flight suit and then looked up. "Do you happen to have a quarter?" she asked the bewildered guard.

He puffed out his chest. "I was raised to not hit girls. But if you don't leave right now, I'll make an exception." The guard gave a dismissive flick of his wrist. "And take your smartass boyfriend with you."

"We don't have time for this," Cyndi said curtly. She turned to Lance. "We're a crew. We'll handle it together." She held out her hand. "Deal?"

"Deal," Lance said, while shaking Cyndi's hand.

In seconds, the guard lay unconscious on the floor after getting an unwelcomed introduction to their martial arts skills.

# CHAPTER 46

THEY STEPPED OVER the man's limp body and ran to the end of the hall. Cyndi and Lance burst into the outer office.

"Where is General McNeil?" Cyndi shouted. "We have to talk to him right away. It's a matter of life and death."

Startled by their tattered appearance and sudden intrusion, Lola Crawford jumped up from her desk. "Who do you think you are busting in here like this? Get out of the general's office right now!"

Cyndi stepped up to her desk. "You don't understand," she pleaded. "We have to see the general. A missile—"

"Miss Crawford, what the hell is going on out there?" McNeil's voice boomed over the intercom box.

She pushed a switch on the intercom. "I have no idea. These two lunatics came busting into the office demanding to see you."

"Go to the lobby and get my guard," McNeil ordered.

"Yes, sir." Crawford dashed out the door, slamming it closed behind her.

The door to McNeil's inner office banged open. The diminutive man stomped out of his office like an angry rooster spoiling for a fight. He yanked the cigar from his mouth. "How dare you interrupt me like this. Who do you think you are?"

Cyndi spun around and faced the general.

He stopped in his tracks with his jaw hanging slack. Brigadier General Arthur McNeil looked as if he'd seen a ghost.

# CHAPTER 47

"THANK GOODNESS WE finally reached you. Sir, I'm Capt. Cyndi Stafford, the crew commander from site Alpha One."

"Aren't you the one who called me? Said there was an emergency?"

"Yes, sir."

McNeil's eyes darted to the door leading out of his office. Beads of sweat formed on his upper lip. "What the hell are you doing here? I ordered you to defend the site."

"Yes, sir, you did. But—"

"You abandoned a nuclear missile and its launch control center that was under attack by a madman?" McNeil looked like he was about to stroke at any moment.

Lance stepped forward. "If you'd just let us explain, sir. We didn't have any other—"

"Who the hell are you?"

"Garcia, sir. Lieutenant Garcia. I'm her deputy."

"Please, sir, I'll explain everything," Cyndi pleaded. "But first you have to send a crisis response team out to Alpha One immediately."

The color drained from McNeil's face. "You can't be serious? Are you telling me there is a Broken Arrow incident at the site?"

Cyndi swallowed hard. "Um…I'm afraid it's worse than that. I think this is a potential NUCFLASH situation."

Only once in the nation's history had a NUCFLASH event ever happened. The US had come within two minutes of launching every nuke it had on the USSR because of it. With only a small number of news outlets operating back in that pre-internet era, the Defense Department was able to threaten and bully them into not reporting the incident. Now the commander of the 90th Nuclear Missile Wing had the unwanted distinction of being in charge for the second one—in the age of instant communication.

Air fled from McNeil's lungs like he'd been punched in the gut. Red-hot embers scattered across the floor from his dropped cigar. "What the hell have you done, Stafford?" He stumbled to the desk and grabbed the phone. McNeil punched an autodial button. When the person on the other end picked up, McNeil shouted, "Get Wilmer on the line. This is an emergency!"

"He's not here, General McNeil," Sergeant Morgan replied. "There's been a serious problem at site Alpha One. He left twenty minutes ago to come tell you in person."

"Wilmer knew about this and didn't notify me?" Now McNeil was sure to stroke.

"Yes, sir. He wanted to make sure it wasn't a glitch in the system before bothering you."

McNeil's eyes bulged out. "A glitch! Son, this is a NUCFLASH event. A damned NUCFLASH event!"

"Oh my God." Sergeant Morgan began to hyperventilate. "Oh my—"

"Scramble a crisis response team to Alpha One immediately. Notify Los Alamos. We need their warhead recovery unit."

"Yes, sir. Right away, sir."

"Notify all LCCs to stand down. Take every missile in the wing off alert status." Veins were popping out on McNeil's neck. "And find me Wilmer! Now, dammit!" He slammed the phone down and turned toward Cyndi. "I want to know what the hell happened out there. Why are you standing in my office and not at your LCC?"

Cyndi hesitated, knowing there was no good way to spin the bad news. She took a deep breath. "I know how this looks, but we didn't have any other choice. All comms were down. We had to get back to the base. You're the only person who could stop this."

"Stop what? What did you do?"

Lance held up both hands. "Hold on, sir. We didn't *do* anything. The REACT console went haywire. It sent us a false Emergency Action Message to launch our missile at China. When we wouldn't do it, the console locked us out and tried to launch the missile itself. The damned thing almost started World War III. There must be a bug in the new software. Hell, forget bug. I'd call it a Godzilla in the software."

McNeil threw up his hands. "The console went nuts. It just decided to attack China. You two expect me to believe this…this bullshit?"

"It's true, sir."

"And how might I ask did you stop this rogue computer from ending life as we know it?"

"I shot it."

McNeil marched up to Lance. "Son, I don't know who the hell you think you're talking to. This is the worst catastrophe in the history of this base—hell, the entire Global Strike Command—and you think this is a good time to make a joke?"

"I'm not joking, sir. It's not like I could have just cut the red wire and everything would have been fine. This wasn't some lame movie. The computer was counting down to launch our missile. It was going to nuke one billion innocent people. So, I shot it."

"What about the missile?"

"The warheads are still armed, but the rocket isn't going anywhere," Cyndi replied. "I used a Hellfire missile from one of Major Pierce's helicopters to destroy the site and bury it."

McNeil looked like his head was about to explode. "Stop. Just stop." He massaged his temples with both hands. "What happened to Pierce? You told me he was trying to gain unauthorized entrance to the grounds."

Cyndi walked over to the window and pointed. "He's dead, sir."

McNeil's eyes widened as he took in the sight of the conflagration on the parade field. "You did that?"

"I had a little help, but yes, sir. My dad taught me to fly helicopters. He taught me a lot of things."

McNeil nervously paced the floor as he shook his head. "This is unbelievable. Do you two have the slightest clue how much trouble you're in?"

Cyndi and Lance looked at each other with complete confusion.

"Hold on. Time out, sir," Lance said.

McNeil continued. "You refused to follow an Emergency Action Message. You abandoned an armed nuclear missile under your direct control. You stole an Air Force aircraft. You killed a Delta Force operator. You sabotaged a console and tried to launch a nuclear missile. You—"

"What?" Cyndi barked, her face turning bright red. "We didn't sabotage—"

"It's all beginning to make sense." McNeil stopped pacing. He looked directly at Cyndi. "You're the one behind this, Stafford. You just tried to nuke China."

# CHAPTER 48

"WHAT THE HELL are you talking about?" she bellowed.

Lance had to restrain Cyndi before she could throttle the general.

"I had nothing to do with this! We stopped the attack!" She struggled to get out of Lance's grasp. "Let go of me! He's lying!"

Lance refused to let her go out of fear that Cyndi would rip the general's head off after his astonishing accusation. "Calm down, dammit. Let's find out what he's talking about." With Cyndi still encircled by his muscular arms, Lance said, "Sir, I don't know what is going on here, but we had nothing to do with this. There's a bug in the software."

"You really believe that, Lieutenant?"

Lance relaxed his grip a little. "Yes. Cyndi and I saw it with our own eyes."

McNeil paused. "Are you always in the habit of addressing higher ranking officers by their first names, Lieutenant Garcia?" He tilted his head and narrowed his eyes. "Is there something more going on between you two than just being a missile crew?"

Cyndi and Lance broke eye contact with the general. Lance loosened his grip on her.

McNeil laughed. "Son, don't tell me you fell for the oldest trick in the book. A beautiful woman says she cares about you, and you throw all common sense out the window."

Lance let go and pulled back. "No, that's not it at all. Cyndi...I mean, Captain Stafford just saved the world from Armageddon. Wyoming would be glowing in the dark for the next ten thousand years if it weren't for her."

"This ridiculous explanation coming from such a reliable source as her lovestruck boyfriend, of course. How convenient."

"It's true. I was there."

"Wise up, Son, it wasn't a bug. The new software must have been deliberately designed to launch your missile no matter what you did." McNeil tapped the side of his head. "Think, Garcia, think. Captain Stafford wrote the procedure manual for the new LCC. She and Dr. Zhao spent months designing the launch software. Either one of them could have doctored the code. God knows Dr. Zhao certainly had enough motivation to go along with her traitorous scheme after what those savages did to his family."

Lance's eyes narrowed. "Why would she do that? She's the number one combat crew commander in the entire wing. She has a spotless service record. Captain Stafford doesn't have any axes to grind."

"Obviously, you don't know her as well as you think." McNeil headed for his office door. He pointed at the floor. "Stay right where you are." McNeil entered his inner office and began rifling through the drawers in his desk.

Lance grabbed Cyndi as she started toward McNeil's office. "Wait. We need to—"

"Let go of me!" Cyndi reared back and delivered an elbow strike to Lance's ribs.

Pain tore through his abdomen as his already cracked ribs absorbed the sharp blow. Lance let go of her and doubled over, clutching his chest. When Cyndi started to walk away, Lance lunged and grabbed her wrist. "Wait," he struggled to say through gritted teeth. "What is he talking about? Why did he…" Lance winced in pain. "Why did he accuse you of being behind all this?"

"I have no idea," Cyndi shot back. She yanked her wrist free from his weakening grasp. "He's lying. What possible reason would I have to do such a horrible thing?"

McNeil emerged from his office holding a folder. He opened it up. "Plenty of reasons, it turns out."

# CHAPTER 49

M CNEIL TAPPED THE documents in the folder. "I did quite a bit of research on you, Captain Stafford. I wasn't about to trust the new Alpha design to just any commander. I thought I'd found the right person. Obviously, I was wrong. The more I dug into your past, the more concerned I became. So, I called in a few favors from friends in Washington. The last details from your background investigation by the CIA came in this morning."

Cyndi's jaw dropped. "You had me investigated by the CIA?"

"Is that surprise I hear in your voice, Captain Stafford?" McNeil looked at her with a smug grin. "Or…could it be the sound a traitor makes just before being exposed?" He pulled a sheet out from the folder and began reading. "Graduated top of your class from missileer school. Expert helicopter pilot. Black belt in several different martial arts. Expert marksman."

"Anyone with a cell phone could have Googled me and found that out," Cyndi said in her defense. "It doesn't mean a damned thing. Why would I want to launch a nuclear missile?"

"For revenge."

McNeil let the incendiary words hang in the air like a bad odor.

"It's the strongest motivation of all."

Lance straightened up, still clutching his ribs. He cocked his head and peered at Cyndi with apprehension. "What is he talking about? Revenge for what?"

"I don't know!" Cyndi pleaded. "I swear, I had nothing to do with this!"

"Your record paints a much different picture, Captain Stafford." McNeil ran his finger across the page as he read. "It says here you were kicked out of pilot training by the base commander himself. According to him, you were a danger to yourself and others."

"He tried to rape me!"

"So, there must be a police report, correct? A harassment complaint? Something in your record that would corroborate your story?"

"It's not a story! He…I…It would have been his word against mine." Cyndi turned to Lance. "It happened!"

Lance listened but didn't respond.

"Then you accused the accident board that investigated your dad's crash of a cover-up." He craned his neck forward and looked more closely at the page. "Well, isn't this interesting. According to you, it wasn't your dad's fault he crashed a perfectly good $300 million jet. No, of course not. According to you, there was a bug in the flight software. Yet not a single accident investigator concluded that a problem with the software was responsible for the accident." He looked out over the top of the folder. "Please, another bug in the software? You two could have been a little more original when you concocted your story for what happened out there today."

"Crappy software happens all the time," Lance volunteered. "My laptop crashed just last week because of a problem with Microsoft Windows. And that software is older than I am."

McNeil ignored Lance and flipped the page. "This is where your report gets most troubling. Your baseless claims of a cover-up became so outrageous that the general in charge ordered you to have a psychiatric evaluation by an Air Force doctor. For paranoia."

# CHAPTER 50

"HE DID THAT to try and get me to back off," Cyndi fired back. "That's one of the devious retaliation tactics that powerful people use when they can't handle having their decisions challenged. They weaponize the mental health system to silence their critics. He was trying to ruin my reputation and discredit my allegations."

"So, the psychiatrist, he was conspiring against you, too?" McNeil said mockingly.

"That Air Force quack wasn't about to torpedo his career. He told the general what he wanted to hear. I went to three different civilian psychiatrists on my own. They all said the same thing. I was one of the sanest, most well-grounded patients they'd ever examined."

"I don't care what they said. You are a disgrace to this command and all missileers."

Lance stepped forward. "Excuse me, sir. I have to speak up. Look, I know you outrank me by a million miles, but you're wrong. Captain Stafford is the best damned missileer the Air Force has. Her willingness to spend day after day in a dank, claustrophobic cave and accept full responsibility for firing the *bullet* without any control over the *gun* or even why it's being fired, proves she is the perfect role model for missileers.

"I'm the one who refused to follow the launch order, not her. She was going to shoot me for not doing my job. That's how dedicated to the mission she is." Lance cleared his throat. "I don't think I've ever said anything so…so illogical, but the fact she wouldn't pull the trigger—in either situation—proves she is the least crazy of us all. I don't care what you or that report says. I believe Cyndi."

McNeil looked at Lance and shook his head. "Gullible to the very end. How noble of you. Maybe if you heard it in her own words, you'd change your mind."

"What do you mean?"

"Two years ago, your *girlfriend* took herself off active missileer status for an entire month for what she herself described as"—McNeil rested his finger on the page and read directly from the report—"being emotionally unfit to be in command of a nuclear weapon."

The walls of the spacious office felt like they were closing in on Cyndi. Her heart began to race. "My dad had just died," she cried out. "Of course I was upset. Who wouldn't be after losing a parent? I needed time off to help my mom settle his affairs after the funeral. I was trying to do the right thing by taking myself off active status!"

McNeil appeared unmoved by her explanation. "I'll be leading the investigation during your court-martial. The resources of the entire US military will be at my disposal. All these sordid details from your past will be presented front and center at the trial. Trust me, neither of you will ever see the outside of a prison for the rest of your lives." He turned to Lance. "Congratulations, Son, she just destroyed your future."

Cyndi was close to tears. "He's twisting everything around. They're just circumstantial, random events from my life. They don't prove a thing. I didn't do this, dammit!" She balled up her fists. "I'll have my day in court. I'll prove you're wrong about me. You're not going to get away with framing me for this."

"And how do you propose to stop me?" McNeil said

tauntingly. "The same way you silenced your coconspir-
ator, Dr. Zhao?"

Cyndi recoiled back. "Dr. Zhao? What the hell are you
talking about?"

McNeil stabbed his finger toward Cyndi. "You killed
him; that's what I'm talking about!"

# CHAPTER 51

"WHOA, HOLD ON a minute," Lance said with his hands raised. "I saw him leave on the helicopter with my own eyes on the monitor in the LCC. Cyndi couldn't have—"

"Three hours ago, I got word that Dr. Zhao's helicopter was missing," McNeil said. "The GEOSAR satellite picked up a distress signal from the emergency locator transmitter. Search teams found the crash site an hour later. There were no survivors." McNeil closed the folder. "How did you do it, Captain? You're a helicopter expert. Did you sabotage his helicopter somehow? Maybe you planted a bomb on board? I gotta hand it to you, Stafford"—McNeil gestured toward the parade field—"you're doing a hell of a job covering your tracks."

Cyndi's eyes filled with fire. "I could say the same thing about you, General McNeil."

"I'd caution you to be very careful with what you say," McNeil growled. "You're already in enough trouble. Threatening a general is hardly going to help."

"Major Pierce said you sent him out to Alpha One to secure the site and bring us back. But the sergeant at command post just said Colonel Wilmer hadn't told you there was a problem yet."

Beads of perspiration formed on McNeil's forehead. He wiped them away with the back of his hand. "I already told you, that lunatic went rogue. I had nothing to do with it."

"Then Pierce tried to kill us. We show up in your office, and you act surprised to see me." Cyndi advanced toward McNeil. "What's the real story? Did you send him there to rescue us or kill us?"

McNeil went toe to toe with her. "Back the hell up, Captain. Now."

Lance grabbed her by the arm. "Cyndi, don't."

Cyndi yanked her arm free.

She spread her feet shoulder width apart.

Her hands came up in front of her.

Cyndi filled her lungs with a deep, oxygenating breath. Then she stepped back.

Clueless as to how close he came to having his neck snapped, McNeil turned to Lance. With disdain dripping from his voice, he asked, "Do you *trust* your crew commander?"

Lance stood next to Cyndi and draped his arm across her shoulders. "With my life. *Sir.*"

"Did she happen to mention that she knows Major Pierce? In fact, knows him quite intimately."

Lance looked at her with a perplexed expression. "Is that true?"

"Wait, I can explain." Cyndi felt as if a noose was being cinched up around her neck.

McNeil pulled an 8x10 black-and-white photograph from the folder. He handed it to Lance.

He examined the photo then thrust it back at McNeil. "This doesn't prove anything. Those two people could be anyone."

McNeil pulled out a second photo. Unlike the first one taken from across the park, this picture was a close-up of a handsome couple sitting together on a park bench, taken with a powerful telephoto lens. He held it up for them to see.

Cyndi and Pierce were holding hands.

# CHAPTER 52

LANCE'S ARM FELL from Cyndi's shoulder. He moved away from her. "What is going on here? Why does General McNeil have a photo of you and Pierce together?"

"Please, let me explain," Cyndi said as she reached out for Lance.

He pushed her hand away and increased the distance between them. "Just…don't. Don't touch me. I want to know why you are holding hands with the lunatic who just tried to murder us."

Cyndi snatched the photo out of McNeil's hand. "This picture was taken years ago. Look at it." She handed it to Lance. "I was just a kid."

He held the photo up to his face. Lance lifted his eyes and glanced suspiciously at Cyndi then back at the picture.

"I was nineteen, living in Israel with my folks." Cyndi's expression saddened. "I was a lonely teenage girl in a strange country with no idea what I was going to do with my life. Pierce was a handsome American." Her head sagged down. "It just happened."

"Then who took this photo?"

"The CIA," McNeil interjected.

"Why would the CIA be following a teenage girl?"

"Not her, you idiot. Pierce was training with Mossad in Israel. You don't get to be a member of the most secretive Special Ops unit in the world and then expect your social life to be private. When young, inexperienced operators are in a foreign country, they're under surveillance every minute of every day to avoid being snared in a honey trap."

"I swear, I never knew Pierce was with Delta Force," Cyndi explained. "He told me he worked for a software company in Tel Aviv."

"But why didn't you tell me you knew Pierce when he showed up at Alpha One?" he asked, confusion blanketing Lance's face.

"I thought he was a programmer, not a trained killer. Besides, there must be dozens of people in the service named Pierce. I couldn't be sure it was him. He was wearing sunglasses at the front gate. Until he tried to kill us in the silo, I never got a clear view of his face."

Lance stroked his chin as he paced the floor. "Something's not right. This doesn't add up. Pierce would have known it was you."

Cyndi's body wilted at his observation. "That jerk didn't even recognize me. Obviously, I was nothing more than a momentary distraction for him in Israel. He stole my innocence, then he dumped me two weeks later for a local girl." Her voice cracked. "I never heard from him again."

Lance went over to Cyndi. He reached out for her hands.

She took them but continued to stare at the floor. "I should have said something, even if I wasn't positive it was him. I'm sorry."

Lance pulled her close and wrapped her arms around his waist. A smirk formed on his face. "You'll probably find this hard to believe, but I've had my heart broken, too. More than once. Besides, you hardly had time to recite every detail from your secret teenage diary. We were a little busy trying not to die."

Cyndi looked up with tears in her crystal-blue eyes.

The hint of a smile appeared. "Thanks, Ice Man." She gave him a gentle kiss.

"Are you really that *blinded* by her beauty?" McNeil asked, shaking his head. "Wake up, Garcia. The evidence is overwhelming. The only possible way you're going to avoid a life sentence is to do the right thing. Cooperate and all this goes away."

"What are you talking about?" Lance shot back.

"Stafford is the crew commander, not you. She's responsible for what happened. Do the smart thing and say that in court and you get your future back." McNeil made wide, animated hand gestures as he spoke. "You want out of the missileer field? Name your dream job." He snapped his fingers. "Done. It's yours. If…you make the correct decision."

Lance released Cyndi from his embrace. "Are you telling me to lie?"

"You're young, Garcia, you have your whole life in front of you. Do you want to spend the rest of it locked up in solitary confinement while you slowly go insane?"

Lance stepped away from Cyndi. "No, of course not. But we're a crew. We did this together, and we're going to fight this together. We're going to win. You'll see."

"Are you willing to risk your freedom on beating a one-star general in a military courtroom?" McNeil said condescendingly. He crossed his arms and waited for an answer.

Lance didn't respond. He wrung his hands as he paced the floor.

"He's right."

Lance looked up to see Cyndi staring right at him.

"He's right," she repeated. "I was in command. I'm the one ultimately responsible for what happened at Alpha One, not you." She drew in a deep breath. "Enough damage has been done already. Go to pilot training. Get your wings." Tears streamed down her soft cheeks. "At least one of us will achieve their dream."

Lance's brown eyes watered up. He reached out and took Cyndi by the hand. "You don't have to do this. We can fight this together."

She pulled her hand away. "There is no *we*. I can take care of myself. I don't need your help." Cyndi turned her back on Lance. "Don't be a fool. Take his offer." She began softly sobbing. "That's an order, Lieutenant Garcia."

Lance couldn't breathe. He felt the oxygen being sucked out of his lungs. A malfunctioning launch console that was determined to nuke China and a bloodthirsty Delta Force operator out to murder them suddenly seemed inconsequential compared to making sense of his conflicting emotions. The first woman he'd ever fallen for had just turned her back on him and told him to betray her.

Going to prison would be like being locked in a claustrophobic LCC for the rest of his life.

Going on without Cyndi would be worse.

Lance came up behind her. He reached out to comfort Cyndi but hesitated. He pulled his trembling hands back. Lance swallowed hard. "I'm sorry, Cyndi. I wish it hadn't come to this. The general is right. With the evidence he has, we don't stand a chance in hell of beating this."

"You've finally come to your senses, Garcia," McNeil said. "You won't regret this."

Lance shot daggers at McNeil and shook his head in disgust. He looked back at Cyndi. Her body quivered as she sobbed. "I need to explain why I'm doing this, Cyndi. Please turn around."

"Just go away."

"Please."

Lance waited.

Cyndi didn't move.

"I have to look you in the eyes when I say this. After

that, I'll do whatever you ask."

Cyndi lifted her head and wiped away her tears with the sleeve of her flight suit. Arms tightly crossed, she turned to face Lance. "Make it quick."

"I've dreamed of being a pilot ever since I was a little kid. It's all I've ever wanted to do. That's why I joined the Air Force. That's why I watched *Top Gun* so many times."

"Well, now you have your big chance. You'll forgive me if I don't throw you a party."

Lance shook his head and gritted his teeth. "God! Has anyone ever told you that you can be so infuriating, so damn stubborn, so—"

"I'm stubborn? I'm sure you own plenty of mirrors, pretty boy, try looking in one."

"Get on with it, Son," McNeil barked.

"Yes, sir." He took in a deep breath. "I'm not very good at…" Lance cleared his throat. "What I mean is… Ah hell, in the words of that great philosopher Maverick, 'You never leave your wingman.' We're a crew. You and I are going to take on the Air Force, and we're going to win."

Cyndi's jaw dropped. She leaped into his arms. Tears of joy streamed down her face. She gently cradled his cheeks in her hands and pulled Lance in close for a kiss.

"You son of a bitch!" McNeil roared. "You think you're going to stab me in the back and get away with it? You just dug your own grave, Garcia!"

Lance just shrugged. "Maybe. But six feet under and sixty feet underground feel the same to me—dark and smelly." He winked at Cyndi. "Either way, I'll take my chances."

"I hope she's worth it, Son, because the two of you are going away for life."

"We'll see about that," Cyndi retorted.

McNeil slammed the folder down on the desk. "Forget about what's in here. Do you really think the judge is just going to overlook everything else you traitors did?

You abandoned an armed nuclear missile accessible to anyone driving by. Our top Chinese missile expert is dead because of you. Major Pierce and his entire team are dead! I don't care what kind of fantastic stories you come up with, you're going to lose!"

Cyndi let go of Lance. She turned and faced McNeil. "What did you just say?"

# CHAPTER 53

"YOU HEARD ME!" McNeil said.

Cyndi cocked her head to the side. "How did you know Pierce had a team with him? I never mentioned that when I called you."

"Of course you did. How else would I have known? The extreme stress you were under has obviously damaged your fragile memory."

"Her memory is just fine." Lance turned and addressed the general. "I was standing right next to Cyndi when she made the call. She never said it."

Cyndi's blue eyes opened wide. "Oh my God. How could I have not seen it? It's you. You did this."

"You really are paranoid, Stafford," McNeil huffed.

"That's why you picked me. You set me up to take the blame for all of this." Cyndi's legs suddenly felt weak.

Lance grabbed her and held her up. "We trusted you. We came to you for help. You *bastard*."

"You're the one going to jail, General McNeil," Cyndi said. "For high treason."

He just laughed at her hollow threat. "Not only are you paranoid, Captain, you're hopelessly naïve." McNeil walked over and snatched the picture of President Donovan off the wall. He spit on it then hurled it to the floor, shattering the glass. Next, he swept his arm across Crawford's desk. Her laptop crashed to the floor. Papers scattered across the room.

"What are you doing?" Cyndi shouted.

In an eerily calm voice, McNeil said, "After I provided proof that you were behind this devious plot, you two martial arts experts attacked me. Said you were going to kill me." He picked up a razor-sharp shard of glass and slashed it across his face. A deep gash opened below his right eye. Blood gushed down his cheek. "I had to make sure the truth got out, so I fought back valiantly." He kicked over his secretary's chair, denting the wall as it crashed into it. "After a vicious fight, it finally ended. I was victorious, of course."

"You won't get away with this," Cyndi said. "Even if I have to get every lawyer in the Air Force involved, the truth of what you did will all come out in the court-martial."

"I won't allow you to waste taxpayers' money on a baseless fishing expedition," McNeil roared back.

"Allow? Yeah, right. We'll see you in court, *General.*" Lance hooked his arm around Cyndi. They turned to leave.

A folder full of circumstantial incriminating evidence wasn't the only thing that McNeil had retrieved from his desk. He reached around his back and pulled a .38 Special snub-nosed revolver from his waistband.

"There's not going to be a court-martial."

# CHAPTER 54

C YNDI AND LANCE spun around.

McNeil aimed the gun at Cyndi's heart. "You couldn't just be a good airman and fall on the damned grenade, could you? No, you had to cause trouble."

Lance held out both hands. "Put the gun down, sir. We can work this out."

"You had your chance, Garcia." He waved the gun to his right. "Move away from the door."

"You're insane," Cyndi said, still clutching Lance.

McNeil snorted. "Genius is the word that comes to mind. Striking the largest cities in China was a tactically brilliant move. It would've decapitated the entire Chinese Politburo in one strike. Their military would have been decimated. The most dangerous country in the world would have been sent back to the Stone Age, where it belongs."

Lance stepped in front of Cyndi. "If you so much as scratch her, I'll…"

"What, kill me? In case you haven't noticed, I'm the one with the gun. Adding two more chumps to my body count won't bother me a bit. And I have the perfect alibi. An open-and-shut case of self-defense if there ever was one."

"I knew it," Cyndi said, shaking her head. "How did you con Pierce and Dr. Zhao into going along with your insane plan?"

McNeil grunted with a self-assured grin. "Ever read

a history book? Revenge isn't just the strongest motivation; it's also the easiest to manipulate. Why do you think I targeted them? They were more than willing to go along with my plan."

Lance started toward McNeil.

"Get back!" he screamed.

Cyndi grabbed Lance's arm. "No!"

McNeil cocked the hammer. "Say hello to your father, Stafford." He sighted down the barrel and started to squeeze the trigger.

Suddenly, the office door crashed open. The window shattered.

A dozen heavily armed security forces stormed in, their M4 carbines raised to the firing position.

The team leader, 1st Lt. Tommy Norris—a tough Nebraska farm kid who once captured an entire Taliban platoon on one of his many deployments—saw McNeil holding a revolver and drew his M9 pistol. "Drop the gun!"

"Shoot him!" Cyndi screamed, pointing at McNeil. "He was going to murder us!"

"Lower your weapon, Lieutenant!" McNeil ordered the team leader, pointing his finger in his direction. He kept his .38 pointed at Cyndi. "These traitors attacked me! Shoot them! Now! That's a direct order!"

Half the airmen trained their rifles on Cyndi and Lance, half on General McNeil.

Norris swung his gun toward Cyndi.

"He's the traitor, not us!" Cyndi pleaded.

Lola Crawford darted into the office. She pointed at Cyndi and Lance. "That's them. Those are the two lunatics who burst into my office yelling crazy nonsense."

"Shoot them, dammit!" McNeil bellowed.

The team leader shifted his pistol back and forth. Confusion pummeled his synapses. "Everyone shut up!" He swung it back and kept his gun aimed at McNeil. "Put your gun down, sir. I need to figure out what the hell is happening here. Lower your weapon."

McNeil glanced sideways. He was looking straight down the barrel of Norris's Beretta. He turned back and sighted down his .38 at the center of Cyndi's chest. His finger tightened around the trigger.

"Don't do it!" the lieutenant screamed.

# CHAPTER 55

ALL TWELVE RIFLES swung toward McNeil.
"I'll sort all this out after my men are safe," Norris said. "This is your last warning, General. Gun down, now."

All eyes were on McNeil.

Heavy breathing from the amped-up airmen was the only sound in the room.

McNeil squinted and considered the overwhelming firepower aimed his way. "Of course, no problem." He thumbed the hammer and slowly returned it to the safety position. "You have the situation well in hand, Lieutenant. I was holding these violent criminals in my office until you brave men showed up." He laid the .38 down on Crawford's desk and backed away.

The men kept their guns trained on McNeil. Adrenaline coursed through their veins. Their trigger fingers were twitching.

"Stand down, dammit!" McNeil ordered.

They ignored the general and looked to their team leader.

"Lower your weapons," he said.

The men reluctantly complied.

"Sir, what's the situation here? Why did you have them at gunpoint?"

Colonel Wilmer stumbled into the office panting heavily. He bent down and planted his hands on his knees. "General McNeil…" He gulped down three deep breaths. "There's been an emergency at site Alpha One."

"I'm fully aware of what happened, Colonel." He pointed at Cyndi. "They just confessed to sabotaging the site and trying to launch a nuclear missile at China."

"Jesus!" Wilmer gasped.

"He's lying!" Cyndi and Lance shouted out in unison.

"When I attempted to stop them from fleeing, they tried to kill me." McNeil touched his cheek then displayed his bloody hand for everyone to see.

Cyndi and Lance's torn and blood-stained flight suits only served to add more nails to their quickly closing coffins.

"You're missileers, for God's sake," Norris said with disgust. "How could you betray your country like that?"

"He's behind all this!" Cyndi yelled, pointing at McNeil. "He just admitted it. You have to believe me!"

The lieutenant waved his men over. "Handcuff these two. They're under arrest."

A policeman approached Cyndi and pulled handcuffs out of a pouch on his belt. "Hands in front. Wrists together." From memory, he recited, "You have the right to remain silent. If you do say anything, it can—"

"No!" Cyndi had no intention of going quietly. She spun around and delivered a roundhouse kick to the side of his temple. His body went limp as he hit the floor like a bag of wet sand.

In a flash, Lance extended his right leg behind the airman in front of him, grabbed his tactical vest, and shoved with all his might. The man tripped and tumbled backward to the ground.

The remaining airmen sprang into action. They violently tackled Cyndi and Lance.

An all-out brawl erupted. Arms, legs, and fists thrashed wildly about.

The fight was over before it had even started. Cyndi and Lance didn't stand a chance of prevailing against such overwhelming odds.

Moments later, they lay on their backs, pinned down by five men apiece.

The airmen forced their wrists together while the lieutenant handcuffed each of them.

"Get off me!" Cyndi squirmed and kicked, trying to break free.

"Stop resisting!" Norris ordered.

Lance worked a foot loose, kicked out, and caught one of the men in the jaw.

Airmen wrestled his leg back down and lay across his shins to prevent more strikes.

Norris fastened thick iron leg shackles—linked together by heavy chain—to their ankles to prevent Cyndi and Lance from doing any more damage to his team.

The chains clanked and rattled as the security forces hauled Cyndi and Lance up to their feet.

With Cyndi safely restrained, General McNeil marched up to her. "Put these traitors in solitary confinement in the stockade," he barked. "I don't want anyone talking to them or visiting them without my authorization."

"Yes, sir. Take them away," Norris said, waving toward the door.

"You have to believe us," Lance pleaded. "We didn't have anything to do with this." He pointed a threatening finger at Norris. "The only reason you're not a pile of radioactive ash right now is because of us."

"General McNeil *admitted* he was the mastermind just before you arrived," Cyndi implored.

"Stafford has a documented history of paranoia," McNeil said in his defense. He picked up the file. "It's all in here." He tossed it back on the desk. "What's more, Captain Stafford did that." He pointed out the window.

Fire trucks were still dousing the flames in the parade field.

"You said so yourself, didn't you, Stafford?" McNeil

said accusingly.

"I had no other choice," Cyndi pleaded. "Major Pierce was going to kill us!"

"It's not my job to decide who's telling the truth," Norris said. "You'll have a trial in six months. The judge will sort everything out."

"Six months!" Fear radiated from Lance's eyes. "McNeil could have us knocked off before then. He's already killed everyone else who could implicate him."

"I'm sorry, there's nothing else I can do," Norris said with true compassion in his voice. "I have my orders." He pointed at the door. "Take them away."

*This can't be happening*, Cyndi thought. Panic swamped her senses. Her heart beat in her chest like a jackhammer.

Everything she'd worked so hard for, all her achievements, were being stolen from her.

So what if her dad had been demanding and her mother could be challenging to get along with? So what if she only had her mom left? So what if she was never going to be a fighter pilot? Life wasn't perfect. She could learn to deal with it. These issues paled in comparison to what was happening. Cyndi Stafford was about to receive a death sentence for something she didn't do. And she was powerless to stop it.

"Please! You can't do this!" Cyndi screamed as the airmen grabbed her arms.

# CHAPTER 56

"WAIT."

All eyes turned to Lola Crawford.

She stayed fixated on Cyndi. She saw the desperation in her eyes. "Hold on, Captain." Crawford gestured toward the parade field. "Did you say Major Pierce?"

"Yes," Cyndi replied. "He's a lunatic. He came out to Alpha One to kill us. He said General McNeil sent him."

"He's a lunatic all right." Crawford shivered at recalling their earlier encounter. "Pierce scared the hell out of me, and all he wanted me to do was get the general for him."

"See, they did know each other," Lance pointed out.

"Norris, I ordered you to take these two to the stockade," McNeil barked.

"I heard you, sir," Norris said, trying to keep his cool.

"Then do it, dammit!"

Crawford blocked the door. "Wait, I can prove who's telling the truth."

"How could you possibly know?" Norris said. "You weren't in the room."

"Because it's on tape."

"What?" McNeil's face turned ghostly white.

Crawford pointed at the ceiling.

The tiny red light on the smoke detector cover was blinking.

"My friend Oliver secretly installed a tiny video camera in the smoke detector. That's why he stopped by once a week, to change the batteries in it. The recordings are stored in my cloud account."

"Why would you do that?" Norris asked suspiciously, looking up at the ceiling.

Crawford planted her hands on her curvaceous hips and glared at McNeil. "I wasn't about to let this jerk sexually harass me again and get away with it. Next time, I'd have proof. With everything on tape, he couldn't lie his way out of it like he did before." She directed a contemptuous grin his way. "Pretty smart of me, wouldn't you say, *Arthur?*"

"You conniving *bitch*," McNeil growled. "I should have fired your ass months ago!"

"So, it *was* you," Colonel Wilmer said from the back of the room.

"Shut up, Colonel!" McNeil shouted.

"Take their cuffs off, Lieutenant," Wilmer said, pointing at Cyndi and Lance. "Arrest General McNeil."

Norris lifted a flap on his belt and pulled out a key to unlock the cuffs.

McNeil suddenly lunged for the .38 Special on the desk. "I'll kill all of you!"

Cyndi spun and broke free from the grasp of the security police. She raised her shackled fists and slammed them down on McNeil's left forearm as he reached for the gun. His ulna bone broke in two with a sickening crack.

The gun fell to the floor. Cyndi kicked it away.

McNeil went down on one knee and screamed in agony as he cradled his fractured forearm.

"Still think I'm just a yoga instructor?" Cyndi said mockingly, glaring down at McNeil. She turned to Norris. "He's all yours."

"You can't do this to me!" McNeil struggled to get to his feet. He was practically foaming at the mouth. "I'll have every one of you locked up for this! I'm the commander of this base!"

"Not anymore." Wilmer stepped forward. "You are clearly unfit to control nuclear weapons. I'm relieving you of command as of now. You're under arrest."

McNeil remained defiant till the bitter end. "You back-stabbing son of a bitch. You'll be dead by the end of the day, Colonel Wilmer. Just like Dr. Zhao. Just like Major Pierce. I got them, and I'll get you, too!"

With a team of security policemen protecting him, Wilmer got up the nerve to say, "Kiss my ass." He turned up his nose. "And it's *General* Wilmer to you."

Norris directed his men to remove the restraints on Cyndi and Lance. After that was done, he took a pair of cuffs and approached McNeil. "You are a disgrace to the uniform and everything it stands for." He roughly grabbed the general's good arm and slapped a handcuff around his wrist. Norris was no less aggressive with his broken arm.

McNeil yelped in pain as the last shackle was clamped down on his wrist. Spittle flew from his mouth as he shouted, "I did what any patriot would do!" He pounded the wall of medals on his chest with a closed fist. "I'd bleed on the damned flag if that's what it took to keep the stripes red!"

His sanctimony enraged Cyndi. She glared at McNeil and pointed a finger right in his face. "Don't you dare call yourself a patriot. You're no different from every other tyrant willing to murder innocent civilians to achieve his agenda. The oath you took when you joined the Air Force means something. That uniform you wear *means* something. It's not about how many medals you wear on the outside. It's about the mettle of the person wearing it. You don't have the courage or integrity to wear anything other than a prison jumpsuit."

"Take him to the stockade," Wilmer ordered. "Put him in solitary."

General McNeil wasn't about to go willingly. It took

two men on each arm to forcefully drag him from the office. As he was being led down the hall, he screamed out supposed justifications for his deranged plan. Everyone from spineless politicians to greedy CEOs who'd sell out America if it meant a quick buck to China killing millions of innocent people by unleashing the COVID-19 virus on the world were included on his list of culprits. His last outburst was, "You'll be sorry; mark my words!"

Wilmer, Crawford, Cyndi, and Lance looked at each other, trying to make sense out of the last few bizarre minutes.

Before anyone could speak, the radio clipped to Wilmer's belt went off.

"Colonel Wilmer, this is command post. How do you read?"

He lifted the radio to his mouth. "This is Wilmer, go ahead."

"Sir, all the other launch control centers tested good. No anomalies found. All missiles are offline."

"Copy that. As I suspected, my command post wasn't the source of the problem. Stand down until you hear from me." He clipped the radio back onto his belt.

Lance nudged Cyndi and rolled his eyes. They each rubbed their wrists to get the circulation going again.

Cyndi went over to Crawford and smothered her in a hug. "Thank you. We owe you our lives—literally."

Crawford squeezed her tightly. "No thanks needed, honey. It felt good finally putting that jackass in his place. Behind bars."

"That was very clever, Miss Crawford," Wilmer said. "Installing a camera in the smoke detector was a brilliant idea. Without that, McNeil never would have confessed."

"Um…thanks," Crawford said quietly. Her head dropped. Her eyes searched the floor. "Yeah…about that."

"About *what*, Miss Crawford?" Wilmer asked suspiciously.

She bit her lip and looked up with an awkward expression. "There's no camera. I made that up. Oliver was just changing the battery every week hoping to get a date. Maybe I should go out with him after all." She winked at them.

Cyndi's eyes opened wide. "What?"

"I had to do *something!*" Crawford replied in her defense. "When I saw the desperation in your eyes, I knew you were telling the truth. Us girls, we have to stick together."

Cyndi thought of Ruby standing up for herself back in the coal mines and nodded approvingly. "Yes, we do."

"This is very troubling," Wilmer said. He paced the floor, deep in thought, and then stopped. "Luckily, there were plenty of witnesses who heard General McNeil confess. I don't see any reason why this information should leave the room. Why don't we just keep this to ourselves?" Wilmer pointed at the ceiling. "And get your friend over here ASAP. Tell him to bring a miniature camera and a dead battery."

"A dead battery?" Crawford asked, looking confused. There was more than enough space in her head for the wheels to turn freely. Her brow furrowed as she thought about Wilmer's suggestion. Suddenly a big smile emerged on her face. She tapped her temple then pointed her finger at Wilmer. "I get it. The dead battery would explain why there's no recording."

"Precisely," Wilmer said, flashing a smug grin.

"Well aren't you the smart one?" Crawford went over and hooked her arm through Wilmer's. Her ample breasts just happened to press up against him. "You're gonna have a lot on your plate after all this, Colonel—excuse me— *General* Wilmer. I happen to be available if you need a clever sidekick."

"No offense intended, Miss Crawford, but"—Wilmer unfurled her fingers from his arm and backed away— "hell no."

She shrugged. "Can't blame a girl for trying."

Wilmer took an anguished breath and massaged his temples. "General Rayburn is going to have a coronary when he hears what happened. His pet project is guaranteed to be canceled after all this." He swallowed hard. "Heads are going to roll." Wilmer's eyes narrowed. He turned and shot a sideways glance at Cyndi.

A startled look flashed across her face. "Why are you looking at me?"

"You *were* the one in command out there," Wilmer said sheepishly.

"Don't even think about it, Wilmer." Crawford stepped between the two. "If you ask me, Captain Stafford here is the one who deserves a medal. She just saved the world from disaster. Cut her some slack."

Her defense of Cyndi was interrupted by a loud commotion in front of the building. The four hurried over to the window.

News vans had pulled up to the headquarters building. Reporters clutching microphones poured out of the vans and were rushing up the steps and into the lobby. Their cameramen trailed close behind.

"Crap, what am I going to tell those vultures?" Wilmer said under his breath.

"The truth," Cyndi said sternly.

"The truth? Are you crazy?"

"If you don't do it, I will," Cyndi said.

Wilmer nearly choked at hearing her ultimatum.

"As you said, I was the crew commander. It's only right I tell them everything that happened."

Wilmer held both hands up. "Don't be rash. Let's think about this."

"*Everything*," she reiterated, arms tightly crossed. "The taxpayers have a right to know."

"Don't forget about the president," Lance added with a chuckle. "I'm sure he'll want to talk to you personally, sir." Lance slowly shook his head. "Man, I wouldn't want to be in the Oval Office when he calls China and tells them your base almost nuked them."

"But I had nothing to do with this!" Wilmer said in a full panic.

"Welcome to the club," Lance said with a wry smirk.

"I think I might have a solution," Cyndi said.

She proceeded to tell Wilmer everything that had happened at Alpha One. And a way to spin it to his advantage.

Wilmer paced the floor. He mulled over what he'd heard. "Hmm…this just might work." He stroked his chin and thought out loud. "The old, leaking fuel tank suddenly exploded after years of budget cuts that left the ground-based nuclear facilities in dangerous shape. You two had no choice but to evacuate." He smiled and nodded. "I'll seal off the area for a mile in every direction. No one will be allowed anywhere near it. For the protection of the public, of course." General Wilmer snickered. "The best part will be watching the media and the politicians play right into my hands when they panic. When I explain to Rayburn that it will be the perfect opportunity to demand a *huge* increase in his budget to fix these 'problems,' I'm sure he'll overlook everything else that happened." If Wilmer could have reached around and patted himself on the back, no doubt he would have. "And I'll come out of this looking like a genius."

"Aren't you forgetting something?" Crawford said rudely, pointing at Cyndi and Lance.

"Oh yeah, right," Wilmer said. "You two are off the hook. I'll see to that."

"That's it?" Crawford sneered. "After all they did?"

Wilmer looked confused. "What else is there?"

"There's two more things I think I deserve, sir. To express your gratitude for everything I've done for you, Global Strike Command, and world peace, you'll be approving my transfer to Laughlin Air Force Base,"

Cyndi said. "To attend pilot training with Lance." She snatched the file off the desk. "And I keep this."

By this time, Wilmer was willing to do just about anything to get them out of his thinning hair. "Fine. Take it. Miss Crawford draw up the transfer orders."

"I ain't your secretary," she shot back.

"You are now," Wilmer replied. "Have the documents on my desk by the end of the day."

"Yes, sir, General." Crawford gave him an exaggerated salute.

"Get your notepad and come with me, Miss Crawford. Let's get this over with."

She strutted over and opened the office door for him. "After you, General. On the way to the lobby we'll talk about my raise."

Wilmer looked at his new secretary, shook his head, and whined, "I'm going to regret this."

Crawford gleefully hooked his arm and led him down the hall.

Lance went over to Cyndi. "Hell of a day, Captain Stafford."

She sighed heavily. "Hell of a day, Lieutenant Garcia." A slight smile emerged on her pretty face. "The upside is we'll never have to sit alert again. And we didn't have to give a sappy going-away speech at this morning's briefing."

"Trust me, the Air Force doesn't want to hear what I have to say." Lance shook his head. "I can't believe we risked our lives rushing back to the base then walked right into the lion's mouth. I should have known it was him."

"Live and learn," Cyndi said with a rueful tone. "I won't make that mistake again."

"You're welcome, by the way," Lance said smugly.

Cyndi cocked her head in confusion. "For what?"

"For helping you save the world, of course," Lance said

with mock annoyance.

Cyndi planted her hands on her hips. "Has anyone ever told you that you're incredibly humble?"

"Surprisingly, no," Lance answered with a big grin. "Humility is one of my best traits."

Cyndi let the obvious contradiction pass.

"This calls for a celebration," Lance declared. "Dinner is on me. My favorite restaurant."

"Sounds like a plan, Ice Man." Cyndi hoisted the file folder up. "I need to burn this first."

"Where?"

Cyndi wandered over to the window. The firemen were still struggling to get the inferno on the parade field under control.

"There," she said, pointing out the window. A broad smile spread across her face. "I can't think of a more appropriate place."

Lance hooked his arm through Cyndi's and led her toward the door. "Looks like you're going to get a second chance at your dream after all."

Cyndi flashed her most flirtatious smile and gazed into his deep brown eyes. "Speaking of second chances, do you have another spare key?"

Lance stopped and let go of her arm. He had a pained look on his face. His reaction was the opposite of what Cyndi was expecting.

"Yeah, about that. I have a confession to make. When we were eating lunch back at Alpha One, I wasn't completely honest with you. Rocko never said those things about wanting you to move in with us."

"Wait a minute." Cyndi pulled away from him. "Is this sudden change of heart about my past?"

"No, it's not that."

She glared at Lance. "Don't tell me you're afraid to commit to a relationship."

"No, it's not that either." He looked down and shuffled

his feet. "Well, not exactly."

"What is it, then?"

Lance looked up. A goofy grin spread across his face. "Rocko's a dog. Dogs can't talk."

Cyndi rolled her eyes. "Very funny. So, if Rocko didn't say those things about wanting me to move in, who did?"

# AUTHOR'S NOTES

**WANT MORE?** Be the first to know about upcoming book releases, events Dan will be at, and more. Sign up for his email list at: https://danstratmanauthor.com/

Check out Dan's YouTube channel for book trailer videos and his series **Practical Tips for Writers** - *http://bit.ly/YTChannel-AuthorDanStratman*

Follow the Dan Stratman Facebook page: *facebook.com/DanStratmanAuthor*

Please consider leaving a review. Honest reviews are immensely helpful for self-published authors.

# THE CAPT. MARK SMITH SERIES

*MAYDAY* (#1 Best Seller)

*HURRICANE* (4.7 Stars on Amazon)

*BETRAYAL*

# ACKNOWLEDGMENTS

Thank you first and foremost to my beautiful wife, Cyndi. Thanks for being my sounding board, first round editor, and constantly challenging me to be the best writer I am capable of being. I love you more than you will ever know.

Several talented people helped me get my manuscript from a rough first draft to a finished novel. Without their help and suggestions *DEADLY DILEMMA* wouldn't be nearly the book it is.

Thank you to Phil Heffley for reviewing and editing each of my novels. Your advice and input are invaluable. Thanks to Rob Perschau, a veteran newspaper man, for the in-depth review and insightful suggestions. Thanks to my brother, Paul Stratman. Who knew you had such a keen eye for editing? Thank you, Anita Marra Rogers, the newest (and obviously very sharp) member of my Beta reader team.

Thousands of courageous men and women have served thanklessly and at times unseen for many decades preserving peace through deterrence in the missile fields. I thank you for your service.

Three individuals were immensely helpful to me during the research phase. Capt. Pamela "Ace" Blanco-Coca is the archetypal missileer and was very generous with her time educating me on the details of this important job. Monte Watts is known as the guru of all things pertaining to Minuteman missiles and was a wealth of information—both technical as well as some "inside baseball". First Lt. Jon Carkhuff's help navigating the frustrating bureaucracy of the Air Force during my research into the highly classified area of nuclear weapons was invaluable. Thank you one and all.

Words can't describe how indebted I am to my editor, Jason Whited. You've provided me with dozens of invaluable tips about writing well in addition to the intricacies of the English language since I began working with you. Your advice and guidance are irreplaceable in helping my writing shine. I consider you a good friend.

And last but certainly not least, I want to thank my readers. I'm eternally grateful to you for not only buying my books but also for telling so many people how much you enjoy them. Good word of mouth is the best form of praise there is for an author and is greatly appreciated.

Sincerely,

Dan Stratman

# ABOUT THE AUTHOR

Dan Stratman is a # 1 bestselling author and retired major airline Captain with over 40 years of experience in the aviation industry. Before flying for the airlines he was a decorated Air Force pilot. In addition, Captain Stratman is a highly sought-after aviation consultant and a popular aviation spokesperson with the media. He is also a World traveler, having been to 43 countries so far.

Dan has an entrepreneurial side that stretches back many years. He developed the popular air travel app, Airport Life. In addition, he created an eCommerce website, ran an aviation consulting company he founded, and has filed numerous patents for consumer products.

Dan is a volunteer pilot with the Civil Air Patrol, performing search and rescue missions and disaster response flights when called on. In his spare time he enjoys mentoring budding entrepreneurs and volunteering weekly with Habitat for Humanity.

The two things he is most proud of are his long marriage to his lovely wife and his three wonderful kids.